W9-AQY-026

# SEE HOW IT'S MADE

CLOTHES • TOYS • SHOES • FOOD • DRINKS • SKATEBOARDS

DK

DK Publishing

**DID YOU KNOW?**
An object is something made from one or more materials that has been designed to do a particular job.

Mississippi Mills
Public Library

**DK**
LONDON, NEW YORK, MUNICH, MELBOURNE, and DELHI

**Written and edited by** Penny Smith, Lorrie Mack
**Designed by** Clare Harris
**Additional editing** Elinor Greenwood, Deborah Lock, Carrie Love, Fleur Star
**U.S. editor** Margaret Parrish
**Additional design** Hedi Gutt, Karen Hood, Poppy Joslin, Sadie Thomas
**DTP designer** Almudena Díaz
**Production** Sarah Jenkins

**Photographer** Gary Ombler

**Jacket designer** Poppy Joslin
**Jacket editor** Mariza O'Keeffe
**Publishing Manager** Susan Leonard
**Managing Art Editor** Rachael Foster

First published in the United States in 2007 by
DK Publishing
375 Hudson Street
New York, New York 10014

Copyright © 2007 Dorling Kindersley Limited

07 08 09 10 11 10 9 8 7 6 5 4 3 2 1
HD120 – 07/07

All rights reserved under Pan-American and International Copyright Conventions. No part of this publication may be reproduced, stored in a retrieval system, or transmitted in any form or by any means, electronic, mechanical, photocopying, recording, or otherwise, without the prior written permission of the copyright owner. Published in Great Britain by Dorling Kindersley Limited.

DK books are available at special discounts when purchased in bulk for sales promotions, premiums, fundraising, or educational use. For details, contact: DK Publishing Special Markets, 375 Hudson Street, New York, New York 10014 SpecialSales@dk.com

A catalog record for this book is available from the Library of Congress.

ISBN: 978-0-75663-204-5

Colour reproduction by GRB Editrice, Italy
Printed and bound by L.E.G.O., Italy

Discover more at
**www.dk.com**

# Contents

Wow! I was made by robots!

DID YOU KNOW?
This book takes you through the manufacturing process of 20 intriguing objects.

see how it's made

>>

# Introduction

**In the bottle factory** machines work 24 hours a day. Two blisteringly hot furnaces melt raw materials into glass. Glass bottles travel along immense conveyor belts. Thirteen production lines make more than 20 million bottles each week.

It's morning. You pull on a T-shirt and drink a glass of apple juice. You do these things without giving them a second thought.

But how is your T-shirt made? And the glass, and the apple juice, for that matter… This book answers these questions and many more about the things that you use all the time.

So many surprising ingredients and so much thought, work, and special equipment go into making everyday things. Did you know that half of a scoop of ice cream is air, that glass is made from melted sand, and that a special robot helps to manufacture plastic toy blocks?

Some things are made in their millions in mass-production factories. Others are made painstakingly by hand, using techniques that have survived many centuries. In the pages of this book, you'll find out about each product's history, its manufacturing methods, and how it has developed into what we use today.

From skateboards to CDs, from ballet shoes to cheese, turn the page to SEE HOW IT'S MADE!

**Only handpicked apples** make quality apple juice (no windfalls allowed!). These are mashed, pulped, and squeezed, then boiled to kill germs. From apples on a tree, to juice in a bottle: 24 hours.

**DID YOU KNOW?**
Hundreds of years ago, most things were made by hand, but today almost everything is mass-produced.

see how it's made

>>

# Oil paint

**Paint is what we use to color our pictures.** But have you ever thought about what it is made of? It's a colorful story...

## Two main ingredients

**1. "Pigment"**—this is what gives the paint its color. Pigments can be natural, such as crushed stone and colored earth, or man-made. The important two things about pigments are that they last a long time and don't fade or change color.

**2. "Binder"**—this is what gives the paint its consistency and texture. It also determines what kind of paint the paint will be. If the binder is oil-based, the paint is oil paint.

**Oil paint**
The modern technique of oil painting was invented by Flemish painter Jan van Eyck around 1410. This is one of his first and best paintings using his new paints—*Portrait of Giovanni Arnolfini and his Wife*, painted in 1434.

*You look beautiful in these new oil paints, my darling!*

There is a huge spectrum of colors, each with its own pigment.

**DID YOU KNOW?**
Oil paints take at least a week to dry. This means an artist can work on his picture day after day to make it just right.

**Here is Jan Van Eyck's secret recipe:**

1. Mix together glass, ash, and mineral pigments.
2. Add linseed oil and stir.
3. Boil the mixture for a long time until thick.
4. Wait until the mixture has cooled.

**Now it's ready!**

*SQUEAL! That's not nice!*

**Oil paints** used to be **stored** in bags made from **pigs'** bladders.

# Some strange ingredients

In the past, oil-paint colors have been made out of some funny things. Here are a few:

**Tyrian purple**, made from the bodies of whelks. Producing 1.5 grams of pigment required 12,000 whelks—making it extremely expensive. Only Roman emperors could afford it.

**Emerald green**, originally made from arsenic— a deadly poison.

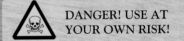

DANGER! USE AT YOUR OWN RISK!

**Indian yellow**, made from the urine of cows fed only on mango leaves in Bengal.

**Early whites**, made from burned animal bones, which produce a gray-white ash.

**Crimson**, made from dried and crushed cochineal beetles (this is still used today).

see how it's made

>>

Artists used to spend **ages** mixing their own **paints.**

start with some gorgeous pigments.

blue          yellow          red

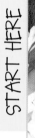

**1  Measure out**  Measuring out the pigment is the first job of the day. Here it is Ultramarine, the most popular blue. This was originally made from a semiprecious stone called lapis lazuli.

**2  Combine**  The pigment will be added to a binder made from linseed oil. This binder will coat the pigment.

**3  Round and round**  Using an industrial mixer, the binder and pigment are mixed together.

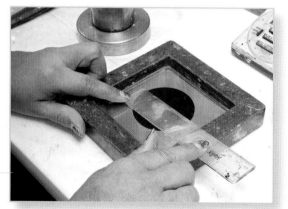

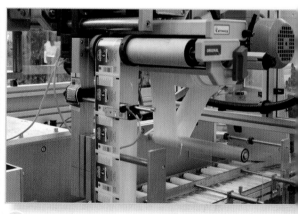

**7  All OK?**  The paint is strictly tested by quality control. A weight is put on a blob of paint so its color and thickness can be checked and the controller can see how far it spreads out.

**8  Roll out the tubes!**  Here you can see empty tubes heading off on a conveyor belt to be filled up with the paint.

**9  Labeling**  The labels are printed on long lengths of paper, then cut and stuck to the tubes.

After the mid-1840s, artists were able to buy **ready-mixed paint** in tubes...

Mix each **pigment** with **binder**.

Put the **paint** **mixture** into a tube and **stick** on a label.

*Hey presto!* You have **colorful tubes** of paint.

**DID YOU KNOW?**
Paint-makers mostly use one pigment for one color. No mixing blue and yellow to make green!

**4** **Pour it out** Next, the mixture is poured into a "milling" machine. Milling of paints makes sure the pigment is spread out evenly and has been done since the 19th century.

**5** **Milling** The color mixture (here it is yellow) is forced between three large, heavy rollers, forcing the oil to "wet" the particles of pigment.

**6** **Moving on** Once the color mixture is milled, it is put into filling machines.

**10** **Seal them up** A special machine seals the end of each paint tube. Seal and go!

**11** **They're ready** The tubes of paint are ready to be packed into boxes and sent off to art-supply stores.

**PRODUCTION TIME**
FROM RAW MATERIALS TO FINISHED PAINT: UP TO 16 HOURS

**12** **Testers** Color strips are painted, dried, and then sent with the tubes of paint so that customers can see the exact colors of the paints.

THE END

... so they could work **outdoors** easily for the first time!

# Ice cream

Nero

**Once upon a time** the Roman emperor Nero wanted a cool fruit dessert. So he sent slaves into the mountains on a mission to bring back snow. On their return, the snow was topped with fruit and the ice-cold dish was served to the emperor.

Marco Polo

**Centuries later** the Italian explorer Marco Polo brought back recipes from his travels in China. These were for frozen creamy puddings, much like the ice cream we know today.

Come on ladies and gentlemen! Get your penny lick here!

**Sweet lickings**
Before the invention of the ice-cream cone, people used to buy glasses of ice cream from street vendors. These cost a penny each, and were called penny licks. After use, the glasses were wiped out with a cloth leaving traces of dirt and saliva. Since they were a public health hazard, penny licks were eventually made illegal.

What's your favorite?

**Edible cone**
In the US, ice-cream cones made their debut at the 1904 St. Louis World's Fair. An ice-cream seller ran out of dishes, so the neighboring waffle maker rolled a waffle into a cone shape. Ice cream was scooped into this—and the ice-cream cone was an instant hit!

Unusual ice cream flavors include green tea, garlic, and bacon.

Mmm.. Fit for a King!

In the 1600s, England's King Charles was served a light, sweet, snowlike dish by his French chef, DeMirco. Charles thought the pudding was so fabulous that he only wanted it served at his royal table. Despite paying the chef to keep the recipe a secret, it leaked out, and now millions of gallons of ice cream are made all around the world.

see how it's made

>>

On average, a cow produces 28–35 pints (16–20 liters) of milk a day.

AT A GLANCE
**ice cream**
**>>**

*My milk is lovely and creamy.*

**Mix** together these **ingredients.**

powdered milk and heavy cream + sugar + dextrose (another kind of sugar) + emulsifier (to stop the mixture from separating)

**peaches** and cream

START HERE

**1** **At the factory** Ice cream is made in huge metal containers. As it is processed, it passes from one to another through pipes.

**2** **Mixing** The ice-cream maker weighs the ingredients. Then he pours them into a blending machine where blades whizz round mixing everything together.

**5** **Resting** Then the ice cream is left in an aging vat to rest and cool down for 12 hours or overnight.

**6** **Tastes good** All flavors, from berries to butterscotch, are added in liquid form. Then the ice cream is whipped to make it light and fluffy, and frozen to make it thick.

**7** **Filling small tubs**
Then the ice cream is pumped into small tubs for one person to eat...

If you let ice cream **thaw** then **refreeze** it...

+ alginade

(to stabilize the ice cream and help it keep its shape)

Then add **flavorings**.

Whip in lots of air and **freeze**.

It's so cool!!

**DID YOU KNOW?** Up to half a scoop of ice cream is air. Without it, ice cream would be more like a solid milky ice cube.

**3** **Pasteurization** The mixture is heated to 162°F (72°C) to kill bacteria and make the ice cream safe to eat. This picture shows a thermograph that records the temperature of the ice cream.

**4** **Making the mixture smooth** The ice cream is then forced through a mesh of tiny holes to break down fat globules. This is called homogenization. It makes the ice cream smooth.

**PRODUCTION TIME**

**FROM RAW INGREDIENTS TO READY: 1 DAY**

THE END

**8** **Filling large tubs** ... and large tubs, for restaurants, hospitals, and schools. On go the lids.

**9** **Final freeze** The ice cream is put into a blast freezer where temperatures are -22°F to -40°F (-30°C to -40°C). Here it is frozen solid.

**10** **At the store** Now it's ready for you. Which flavor will you choose?

...ice **crystals** form, making the **ice cream grainy**.

# Blown glass

**The story of glass** begins with Phoenician sailors camping on a sandy beach. They put their cooking pots on soda rock and lit a fire underneath. The next day they found a clear, hard material by the burned-out fire. This was glass, made when the fire's heat fused the sand and soda together.

**Egyptian glass**
Egyptian craftsmen were among the earliest known to have worked with glass. They made hollow containers by molding bottle shapes from mud and sand, then dipping them into molten glass. When the glass was cold, the craftsmen scraped out the sand. Later the Egyptians learned how to blow glass as shown in this ancient picture.

**Lead crystal**
In 1688 an Englishman, George Ravenscroft, replaced some of the potash in glass with lead oxide. This produced a crystal-clear glass that was great for telescopes and magnifying glasses. The sparkly glass could also be cut and engraved elaborately.

**Beware poison!**
Around 100 years ago a dark blue bottle like this meant the contents was poisonous. Raised ridges, dots, or the word "poison" warned people who picked up the bottle in the dark.

POISON

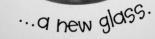
...a new glass.

To make **bottles and glasses** look **identical...**

**How to blow glass** Craftsmen make hollow containers by blowing air into molten glass. They blow through long metal tubes, shaping the glass as they work.

DID YOU KNOW?
When you tap a lead crystal glass with your fingernail, it makes a ringing sound.

see how it's made >>

...blowers shape them in a mold.

Ingredients *include* sand, lead oxide, *and* recycled glass.

recycled glass (called cullet)

lead oxide

These are mixed and then melted.

The glass used here is lead crystal.

sand

START HERE

**1  Gathering glass** A craftsman dips a blowing pipe into a furnace of soft molten glass. He gathers the soft glass on the end of his blowpipe.

**2  Shaping** This yellow-hot glass is called a gob. It's as runny as syrup. The craftsman starts to roll it into the shape of a drinking glass.

**3  First blow** Then he blows hard into the gob. See how it starts to expand like a balloon. He lets the gob cool slightly.

**7  Out comes the glass** Can you see how the bottom is shaped like a tumbler? The top looks more like a bottle. This will be cut off later.

**8  Polishing the glass** The tumbler is now being polished by a flame. This melts away lines and marks left by the mold.

**9  Then into the lehr** The glassmaker snaps the blowpipe off the glass. Then he puts the glass into a cooling tunnel called a lehr. Here the glass gradually cools to room temperature.

Teams of craftsmen *are led by a* master glassblower...

They're **blown** into **Shape** ........ and **polished** ........▶ The **top** is **cracked** off ........

Cheers!

**DID YOU KNOW?**

The temperature is a sizzling 2,550°F (1,400°C) in the furnace.

**4** **Gathering more glass** Then he adds more glass from the furnace. He shapes it with wooden tools and smooths it on a wad of wet newspaper.

**5** **Then into the mold** Now he puts the gob into a mold shaped like a drinking glass.

**6** **Blow again** He blows through the blowpipe into the gob. The gob gets bigger and fills the mold.

**PRODUCTION TIME**

**FROM THE GOB TO FINISHED GLASS: AT LEAST 5 HOURS**

THE END

**10** **Cracking off the top** Next, the glass is held upside down and a diamond is used to cut a line all the way around. Then a fine gas flame heats the line. The glass cracks and falls away.

**11** **Smoothing the rim** No sharp edges are allowed! So the rim of the tumbler is reheated to melt rough edges and then polished.

**12** **Inspection time** The glass is inspected. It has to be perfect to be stamped with the maker's mark. If there is a chip or air bubble it is broken up and sent back to the furnace for recycling.

...He takes **10 years** to perfect his **skill.**

# Pointe shoes

**For classes,** children and young students wear soft ballet shoes made from leather or fabric. For over 150 years though, female professionals have performed in pointe shoes so they can dance on their toes.

**DID YOU KNOW?**
The floury paste used in blocks can contain tiny weevils that appear in warm, damp shoes after months of use.

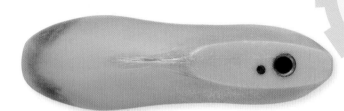

Each pointe shoe is shaped around a LAST that represents the size and shape of a dancer's foot.

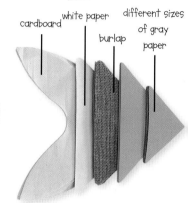

cardboard   white paper   burlap   different sizes of gray paper

## The story so far...

**Dancing shoes with stiffened toes of some kind have been around since about 1810.**

But the real art of using pointes to express grace and weightlessness was perfected by a famous Italian ballerina called **Marie Taglioni** during the 1830s.

Since the days when she wore them to suggest the romantic, magical heroines she portrayed, pointe shoes have been constantly changing in design and construction.

Today, modern versions can support dancers through a fantastic range of dramatic turns and leaps that, even a couple of generations ago, would have been impossible to perform.

The UPPER is made from one layer of satin and two of cotton canvas, all stitched together.

Different materials cut into triangular shapes in decreasing sizes are layered to form the BLOCK.

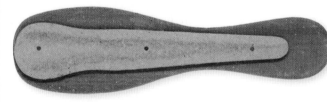

Shoes are strengthened with a rigid INSOLE and SHANK.

FLOUR-AND-WATER PASTE (with a few secret ingredients) sticks the layers together and hardens to give support.

The leather SOLE is stamped with the manufacturer's name.

A thin canvas SOCK lines the finished shoe.

SATIN RIBBONS are about 1 in (2.5 cm) wide and 18 in (50 cm) long.

Ballet dancers use **ribbons** to keep their **shoes on...**

**Upper**
This term refers to all the fabric parts of the shoe, and does not include the sole, insole, shank, and sock.

**DID YOU KNOW?**
Dancers sew on their own ribbons so they can position them precisely, and make sure they're secure.

**Block**
The block covers the toes and provides the support a dancer needs to stand on pointe.

**Side quarters**
The sections of satin from the side seams to the back are called the side quarters.

**Vamp**
The vamp is the part of the upper that extends from the platform to the binding at the center front of the shoe.

**Platform**
This is the outer, flat surface of the block on which the dancer balances.

Because pointe shoes are pink to match the dancer's tights, they help her to create an unbroken line through her legs and feet. This is The Royal Ballet's Tamara Rojo (partnered by Inaki Urlezaga) in *Romeo and Juliet*.

**Most ballet companies** have their own shoe mistress, who is responsible for ordering all the shoes and making sure each dancer has plenty in stock. A female dancer tends to have all her pointe shoes made by one maker, whose shoes suit her particularly well.

**see how it's made**
**≫**

...sometimes they also **glue the backs to their tights!**

AT A GLANCE
pointe shoes
>>

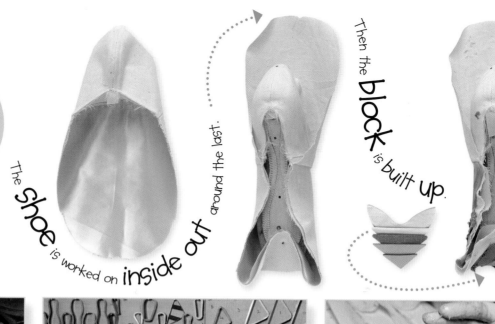

The **shoe** is worked on **inside out** around the last.

Then the **block** is built up.

The upper is stitched to the **sole**

**1** **Ready-made parts** Fabric uppers are assembled at another site and stored at the factory until they're needed. The "satin" is actually a mix of cotton and viscose.

**2** **Skilled eye** One of the clickers cuts out leather soles. Cutting work like this is done mostly by eye, so irregularities in the natural material can be allowed for.

**3** **Getting the shape** A skilled "maker" tacks the sole to the last temporarily. He then shapes the upper around it—inside out—and builds up the block in layers.

**7** **Oven dried** To harden the blocks, the shoes (with lasts) are racked in a warm oven overnight. After this, it takes at least 10 days for them to be fully "cured," or ready for use.

**8** **Marking up** The maker's work is now finished. When the shoes arrive in the binding room, the lasts are removed and the soles are marked with their size and width fitting.

**9** **Measured to fit** Each vamp is measured and marked to the right length for the style required, or for the particular dancer who will wear the shoe.

Before shoes go into the **oven,** their maker puts his **mark** on each **sole.**

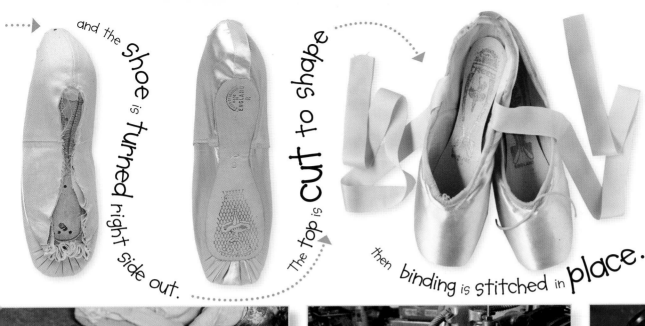

...and the *shoe* is *turned* right side out. The top is *cut to shape* then *binding is stitched in* **place.**

DID YOU KNOW?

The workers who cut out the insoles and the fabric triangles are called "clickers."

**4 Folded to fit** With the shoe still inside out and the last inside, the maker pleats the fabric upper around the block and tacks the pleats down with string.

**5 Machine stitches** The shoe is passed through a special machine that stitches the upper into a groove that runs around the edge of the sole. This anchors the pleats in place.

**6 Final shape** The maker removes the shoe from the last, turns it right side out, then replaces the last and shapes the block and platform before the paste dries and hardens.

**10 Cut to shape** An experienced cutter shapes the shoe's vamp and sides. Aside from the marked vamp, there are no guidelines—the work is done completely by eye.

**11 Bound up** An ingenious machine attaches binding around the edge of the upper and, at the same time, inserts the drawstring that goes through it.

**EVERY YEAR**
**ONE MANUFACTURER TURNS OUT 250,000 PAIRS OF POINTE SHOES.**

**12 Finishing off** Finally, each pointe shoe is neatened up and fitted with a canvas liner, called a sock, which carries the manufacturer's symbol, or logo.

THE END

Shoes for individual **dancers** are made in batches of up to **30 pairs.**

# Sausages

**Sausages are made of ground meat**, fat, herbs, and spices mixed together and fed into casings that hold the sausage in shape. They have been eaten for at least 2,000 years—the Romans enjoyed a huge variety including a blood sausage called *botulus*.

How do you like yours? Grill it, fry it, barbecue it, boil it.

Sausages are mostly made from pig but sometimes they are made from other animals (see below).

### Growing on trees
The fruit of a South African sausage tree looks just like sausages. Each tree bears hundreds of fruit, some as long as 2 ft (60 cm). Although the fruit is inedible to humans, it is a popular food for monkeys and elephants. Native women also make it into a face cream to keep their skin smooth and clear.

## DID YOU KNOW?
English sausages are known as "bangers," probably because of the loud popping sound they make when cooking.

beef

venison

boar

### Vegetarian sausage
Although not strictly a sausage because it doesn't contain meat, this is a popular alternative made from tofu and soybeans.

tofu and vegetables

whole range that are **fresh** and ready to cook. They can be small

\>\>

**Chorizo**
Sold ready to eat, this spicy Spanish sausage is made with pork and chilli pepper.

**Frankfurter**
This sausage is named after the German town where it was first made. It is moist and smooth.

**Black pudding**
This is made mainly of pigs' blood. Other ingredients include fat and oatmeal.

**Bratwurst**
A German sausage made from pork, beef, or veal. Brat means finely chopped meat.

**Liver sausage**
This smooth, spreadable sausage contains pork liver and is sold ready to eat.

**White sausage**
A German Bavarian speciality, this sausage is made from veal, bacon, and lemon. It is cooked in water which turns it this gray-white color.

**Pepperoni**
A spicy Italian sausage with a hard, dry texture, pepperoni is popular on pizzas.

**Salami**
A large, strongly flavored sausage, salami is usually sliced thin and served cold.

sausages, and a dried sausages, smoked sausages, You can buy cooked sausages, finger-size chipolatas, or spirals. cocktail sausages,

Oink, oink!

23

AT A GLANCE
sausages
>>

A pig is raised.

Its meat is **ground.**

pepper

Herbs and spices are added.

salt

basil

START HERE

**1** **Where do they live?** Pigs are raised on farms. They like a warm and comfortable hut to shelter in, but they spend a lot of their time outside, too.

**2** **Fattened up** The sausages shown here are made from pork. So first the pig has to be fed and looked after. Then, when it is big enough, it is killed and becomes meat.

**3** **Cutting up meat** The butcher trims the fat off the meat, then cuts the meat into chunks. A lot of sausages are made from scraps, but this is top-quality meat from the muscle of the pig.

**7** **Mixing and grinding** The butcher mixes everything by hand, pulling the ground meat apart so the ingredients are evenly combined. Then, it's all ground again.

**8** **Fill 'em up** Next he puts the final ground meat mixture into the filling machine, which will feed it into the casings.

**9** **Long tube** A single casing (made from pigs' intestines) is loaded onto a metal tube attached to the filling machine.

One pig contains about **65 ft (20 m)** of intestines...

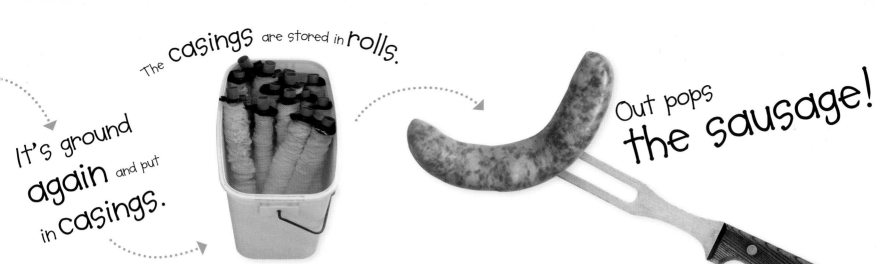

It's ground **again** and put in casings.

The **casings** are stored in **rolls**.

Out pops **the sausage!**

**4** **Grinding machine** The butcher puts the chunks of meat into a metal tray on the grinding machine.

**5** **Ground meat** Blades inside the grinding machine cut the meat into tiny pieces and force it out onto a plastic tray.

**6** **Additional ingredients** Then the butcher adds the other ingredients including onions, herbs, spices, salt, and pepper.

**10** **Filling the casings** Then the ground mixture is forced into the casing, making one very long sausage.

**PRODUCTION TIME**

**FROM MEAT TO SAUSAGES: ABOUT 2 HOURS**

THE END

**11** **Smaller sausages** The butcher twists the sausage every 4 in (10 cm) to make lots of little sausages. He twists these together to make the finished product, ready to be cooked and eaten!

**DID YOU KNOW?** In April 1995, an incredibly long sausage was made in Kitchener, Ontario, Canada. It measured 28 miles (46.3 km).

...that's enough to make over **100** sausages!

# Plastic blocks

**Do you like building** with plastic blocks like these? Since they have studs, these blocks hold together better than smooth blocks. You can turn them into fantastic creations including tall towers, animals, and robots. Then when you've finished, take them apart and build something else!

Amusement parks like the one in this picture attract well over a million visitors a year.

## Building big

Plastic blocks have been used to build huge amusement parks. These are packed with great city scenes, wildlife parks, and massive extinct animals all made from blocks.

This huge technosaurus is made from more than one million plastic blocks.

To build a column to the Moon... ...you'll need to use 40 BILLION plastic blocks.

Wow! That's a lot of blocks.

---

**Strange but true**

Incredibly, there are more than 915 million ways of combining six eight-stud blocks of the same color. Here are some of them. Can you think of any more?

More than **four hundred million** children **and adults...**

DID YOU KNOW?
Over 30,000 blocks and other components are manufactured each minute.

**At the factory machines do the work!** They melt the plastic and mold the blocks. These machines are so accurate that out of every million blocks made, only around 18 are rejected as not good enough. The robot, called "Truck 01" in this picture, collects the blocks once they are molded.

I will obey.

TRUCK01

NXT

8527

**Start with a plastic block** and work your way up to building a robot that you can program to pick things up, walk, and even dance. The parts for this robot are made in a factory—it's a robot made by robots!

see how
it's made

This designer has **great ideas!**

I've a cunning plan.

He **sketches** and tests a design.

Plastic blocks have to be exactly the same size as each other, so they are made by machines.

START HERE

**1  Making sketches** Designers draw lots of sketches of people and buildings that children can make from plastic blocks. Here are designs for a knight and castle.

**2  Detailed design** Then the designer makes careful drawings showing the precise size and shape of each new plastic block.

**6  Out fall the blocks...** Once each block is shaped, it takes about 10 seconds for it to cool and harden and drop out of the machine.

**7  ...And into a box** When the box is full, the molding machine sends a radio signal to a robot truck.

**8  The robot truck** This automatically trundles to the right box, picks it up, and puts it on a conveyor belt.

Children all over the **world** spend...

The plastic is **melted** and **molded.**

The pieces are **painted** and **stuck** together.

Now it's **play time!**

**3**  **Testing the toy** Before the new blocks are made in the factory they are tested to make sure they are perfect. Here a designer is checking that the pieces fit together.

**4**  **Plastic granules** Molded blocks are made from colored plastic granules. These are heated to a sweltering 450°F (232°C) so they melt.

**5**  **Molding blocks** The melted granules are poured into block-shaped molds. Then molds like the ones shown here are pushed into the soft plastic to make the insides of the blocks.

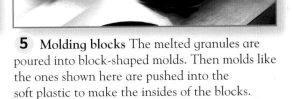

WORLDWIDE
**OVER 500 PLASTIC COMPONENTS ARE MADE EACH SECOND.**

THE END

DID YOU KNOW?
Enough plastic blocks have been made for each person in the world to own 62 of them.

**9**  **Adding the detail** Next stop is the assembly halls where blocks and other plastic shapes are decorated with numbers, faces, and clothes. Some of the pieces are stuck together to make little people.

**10**  **For sale** The pieces are packed into boxes, loaded onto trucks, and driven off to stores for sale.

...5 billion hours a year playing with **plastic blocks.**

# Compact discs

**Compact discs are miracles of modern technology.** They provide hours of entertainment and hold huge amounts of digital information—and all on a disc that is only one millimeter thick.

The width of one pit is 700 times smaller than a pinprick.

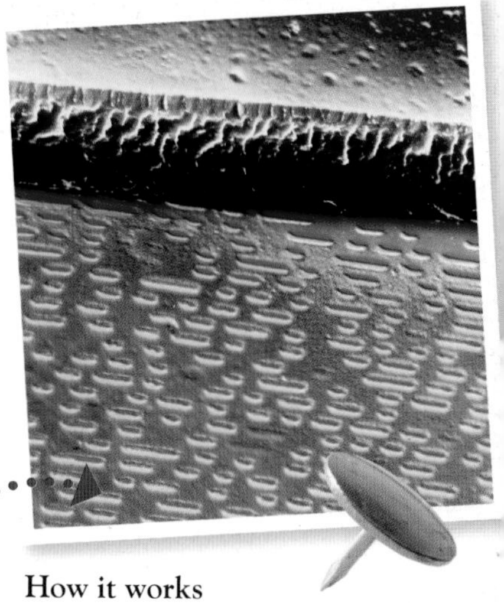

## Invention
The CD was invented in 1980 by a joint task-force of engineers from Philips and Sony electrical companies.

laser beam

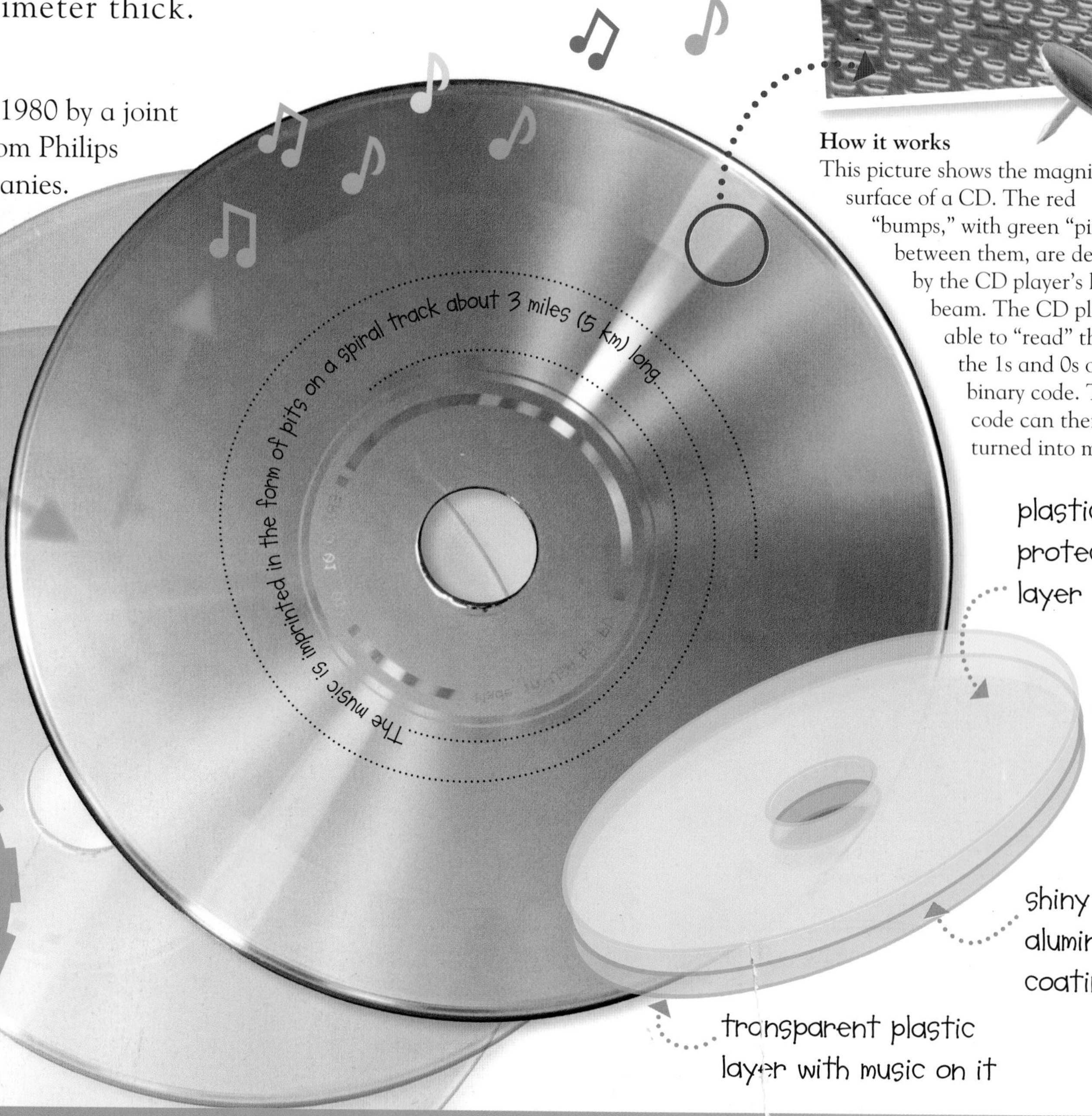

## Play ▶
CDs are read by a CD player's red-light laser beam hitting the tiny pits and bumps on a CD's surface. They play from the center to the edge.

The music is imprinted in the form of pits on a spiral track about 3 miles (5 km) long.

## How it works
This picture shows the magnified surface of a CD. The red "bumps," with green "pits" in between them, are detected by the CD player's laser beam. The CD player is able to "read" this in the 1s and 0s of binary code. The code can then be turned into music.

plastic protective layer

shiny aluminum coating

transparent plastic layer with music on it

## DID YOU KNOW?
The shelf-life of a CD is about 100 years.

CDs **rotate** at a speed of **400 times a minute** at the beginning...

**DID YOU KNOW?**
The data CDs contain is equivalent to 500,000 pages of text—that's eight trees-worth of paper.

**It all starts in the recording studio.** A singer sings into a microphone while an engineer sits at a sound desk in a booth and fine-tunes the sound. Often singers wear headphones. Through these they can hear the backing track—previously recorded instruments and beat—to sing along to. After the recording, all the elements of the song are put together. The song is then ready to be put onto a CD.

**Recycling**
CDs are being thrown away in sparkling mountains. Instead of throwing them out, see if you can recycle them—perhaps give them to friends, or sell them. Some people find them handy as drink coasters!
Here's a hint for scratched CDs: rub toothpaste on the shiny side from the center out. The sticky toothpaste mends minor scratches.

**see how it's made**

**>>**

...and **250 times a minute** at the end (there is more information per rotation on the edge of the CD).

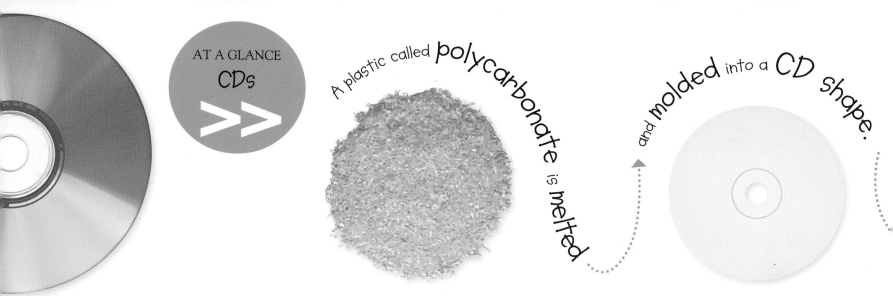

A plastic called **polycarbonate** is melted and molded into a **CD shape**.

START HERE

**1** **At the factory** Here's the CD factory. Let's go inside!

**2** **Making the master** Music is put onto the master CD. All the CDs will be copied from this version, so it must be perfect. It is made inside this air-locked, dust-free cubicle.

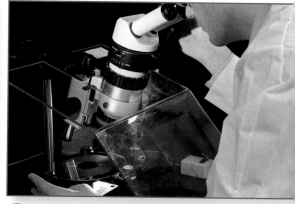

**3** **Taking a close look** The master is checked very carefully before it is copied.

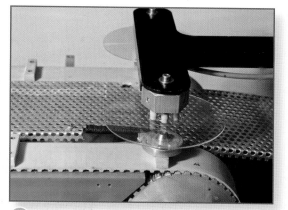

**7** **Moving on** At this stage, the CDs still look like clear plastic. Here is one leaving the machine.

**8** **Shine and protect** Next the CDs are coated in a thin layer of aluminum. Finally they are coated in a protective resin.

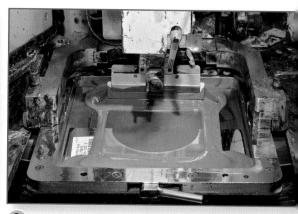

**9** **Add color!** Here's a CD going through the screen printer, which stamps on information about what it contains.

The **shiny surface** of a CD **reflects** a CD player's **red laser**.

Music is stamped onto the CD.

The CD is coated with aluminum, then printed and packed.

See How It's Made
Greatest Hits

DID YOU KNOW?
Stamping a CD with digital information takes only five seconds.

**4** **Into the bath** When the workers know that everything is fine, the master is dunked into a bath of molten nickel to coat the CD.

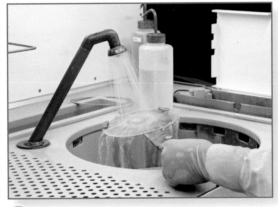

**5** **Now a shower** After the nickel bath, the master is cleaned. It is now called a "stamper".

**6** **Trimming the CDs** This machine trims the stamper so it fits exactly into the next machine— the CD pressing machine. Here it is pressed ito soft plastic CDs, making tiny dents called pits.

PRODUCTION TIME
FROM MAKING THE MASTER TO THE BOXED CD: 10 DAYS

THE END

**10** **They're ready** The CDs and booklets are machine packed into their clear plastic cases. The machine even flips the lid over to close each one.

**11** **At the warehouse** Everything is automatic. This big yellow arm can read barcodes on the boxes of CDs and pick up the ones that are wanted. No need for lugging boxes!

This is what **enables a CD player** to read the **CD.**

# Apple juice

**Delicious apple juice** is made from fresh apples. Apple trees produce flowers every spring, and these flowers become mature apples in the fall. Apple flowers look a bit like roses, which isn't surprising: apple trees belong to the rose family.

We're taking apples from Rome to England.

## Ancient fruit

The apple was the first tree to be grown specially for its fruit. The ancient Romans loved apples, and they originally took apple trees to Britain. Later, apples from Britain were taken to America so seeds could be planted there. In most versions of the story of Adam and Eve, the forbidden fruit the serpent tempted Eve to eat was an apple.

Apple trees can grow to more than **eight times** my height.

Apples are very **healthy**— they're not only FULL of good things like **vitamins** and **fiber**, they also contain no fat, salt, or cholesterol.

**A world of choice**
There are nearly 10,000 varieties of apple, and lots of them get made into juice. They come in all shades of red, green, and yellow; the smallest are a bit bigger than a cherry, while the biggest are larger than a grapefruit.

Decio       Grosse de St.-Clement

**Liquid apples**
In addition to apple juice, apples are used to make apple vinegar and pectin, a substance that makes jam set. When it's fermented, apple juice can become cider, wine, a liquor called applejack, and a strong liqueur called Calvados.

# Juicy fact

Fresh apple juice is good for you. Some experts believe it offers more protection against illness than the fruit itself, because the goodness is more concentrated.

DID YOU KNOW?

Apple trees can produce fruit for more than a hundred years.

Only fresh "table-quality" fruit goes into the juice.

see how it's made

>>

Apples are delivered to the factory in big wooden or plastic crates.

All apples intended for quality juice are hand picked. This means that no windfalls (fruit that has fallen on the ground) and no mechanically harvested fruit is used.

FRUIT DIRECT

FRUIT DIRECT

Start with
an **apple**
tree

and lots of **juicy apples.**

START HERE

**1 Only the best** On a conveyor belt, all the apples are washed and sorted carefully by hand. At this stage, any bruised and blemished fruit is thrown away.

**2 Monster mash** The best fruit—peel and all—is dumped by the conveyor belt into a gigantic masher. This machine turns it into a thick pulp, which is called mash.

**6 Full blown** The plastic bottles are stored as tiny "preforms." When they're needed, they're placed in special molds. Then warm air is forced inside so they stretch and expand.

**7 Fill 'em up** The finished bottles are sterilized to make them very clean, then placed on another conveyor belt so they can be filled with the freshly pressed apple juice.

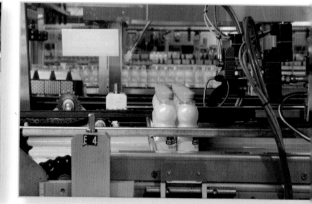

**8 Topped up** When the bottles are full, each one is closed with a plastic cap. A special machine makes sure all the caps are screwed on tightly.

After the **juice** has been squeezed out, the pulp that's left (called pomice) is used for **animal feed.**

Off to the factory...

Take the apples to the factory, where they are **pulped** and the juice is **squeezed**.

Then the bottles are **made** and

**filled up.**

**3** **The big squeeze** In this machine, the mash is forced through a filter inside a fabric tube called a sock. The filtered juice oozes out the sides into the surrounding pipe.

**4** **Fresh and clean** The juice is heated to a very high temperature, then cooled to a low one to kill any bacteria. This process is called pasteurization.

**5** **Perfect every time** To make sure the quality of the juice remains high, a sample is taken from each batch and tested for taste and texture.

**9** **Finishing touches** Each cap is stamped with the date so people will only drink the juice when it's really fresh. After that, bright labels are stuck on all around the bottles.

**10** **Final check** Each bottle is scanned electronically to make sure the cap fits tightly, and that there are no leaks anywhere.

CHECKSTAR

THE END

PRODUCTION TIME
FROM APPLES TO BOTTLED JUICE: ABOUT 24 HOURS

DID YOU KNOW? The science of growing apples is called pomology.

COPELLA APPLE

An apple tree can take up to **five years** to produce its first **fruit.**

>>

After they're filled, the bottles move into the huge packing hall.

<<

Their first stop is the laner, a machine that arranges the massed bottles into single file, ready for the labeling process.

When the bottles are filled, they attract condensation on the outside. To dry them off so labels will stick, they're passed through two air-blowing machines.

**DID YOU KNOW?** Many apple varieties are descended from small, sour crab apples, which still grow wild in many parts of the world.

Sometimes, the labels aren't stuck on quite straight, or they're in the wrong position. These faulty bottles are removed from the line so they can be labeled again.

# Skateboard

**During the 1950s,** California beach surfers wanted to bring surfing to the streets, so they rolled along the sidewalks on homemade boards—often wooden planks with roller-skate wheels underneath. But it wasn't long before big manufacturers were producing the tough, slim models that modern skateboards are based on.

## For successful skating...

... you'll need a good board to achieve speed and lift, plus a helmet and knee- and elbow-pads for safety.

**Waves of cool**
Because skateboarding was invented by surfers, early skaters copied surfing styles and movements. Later, they went on to develop tricks of their own.

Helmet

Slip mat on top

Truck (axle) base

Elbow pad

Knee pad

Tail

Wheel

You need strong leg muscles to make your board spin and jump.

**DID YOU KNOW?**
In its early days, skateboarding was known as "sidewalk surfing."

**High flyer**
The Great Wall of China is so massive, it can be seen from space. Although it is as tall and wide as a house, American skateboarder Danny Way believed he could jump it. So in July 2005 he set off down his skateboarding ramp and leaped in spectacular fashion over the huge wall.

**Ollie up**
To jump up curbs or across gaps, skateboarders often perform an "ollie" (named after its inventor, Alan "Ollie" Gelfand). The magic of this move is that the board appears to stick to the skater's feet in midair. To make this happen, the skater crouches low, pushing down on the back of the board with one foot as he jumps forward. Then he straightens the board with his other foot as it flies through the air.

WHoooooosh!

see how it's made
>>

41

**Seven** sheets of wood are stuck together

then **left** to cure for 3 weeks.

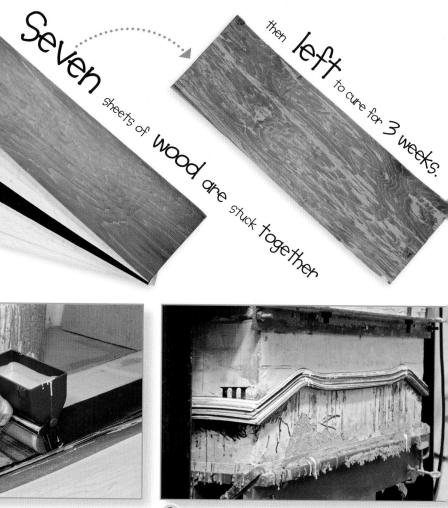

DID YOU KNOW?
The world's longest skateboard was made in Newton, Massachusetts, in 2005. It measures 30 ft (9.15 m).

START HERE

**1 Strength in numbers** This skateboard is made from seven thin sheets of Canadian maple, a very hard wood. The layers are stuck together with craft glue.

**2 Pressed into shape** The glued sheets are fed into a press, which makes them flat in the middle and curved up at each end. The press can take three skateboards at a time.

**6 Cutting out the shape** The maker cuts the skateboard shape out of the layered boards using a band saw with a long steel blade.

**7 Smoothing operator** Then he smooths and rounds the skateboard edges with a powerful rotary sander.

**8 Final finish** Dressed in protective clothing and wearing a mask, a worker sprays lacquer paint on the board.

The pressing machine applies a huge force of **22 tons (20 metric tons)** to the layered sheets of maple.

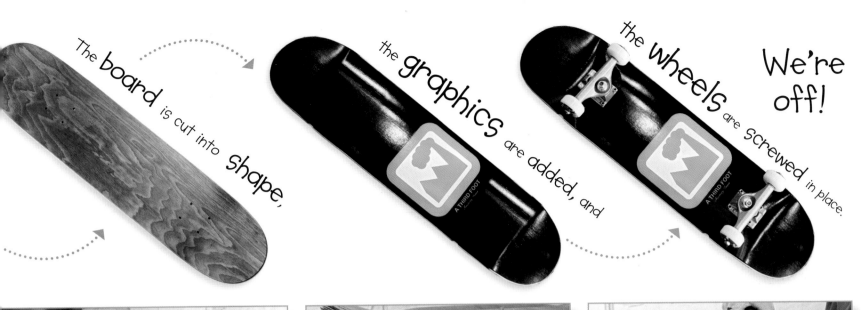

The **board** is cut into **shape**, the **graphics** are added, and the **wheels** are screwed in place. We're off!

**3** **Dry curing** The pressed boards are left in curing stacks for about three weeks so that any excess moisture in the wood will dry out completely.

**4** **Drawing the shape** After the pressed boards are cured, the maker uses a template to draw the shape of the finished skateboard on each one so it can be cut out later.

**5** **Drilling for wheels** Next he drills holes where the wheels will go so they can be attached at the end of the production process.

**9** **Identifying mark** The manufacturer's logo is applied to the skateboard as a transfer. This is done by passing the board between two rollers.

PRODUCTION TIME

FROM MAPLE SHEETS TO FINISHED BOARD: ABOUT THREE WEEKS

THE END

**10** **Ready to roll** Finally, the wheel attachments, called "trucks," and the wheels themselves, are screwed in place on the board.

The top **surface** of a skateboard is called the **"deck."**

# Honey

**If it weren't for bees,** flowers would not get pollinated and we'd have no honey. Here's all about these busy bugs, and their lives' work.

## Bee shapes and sizes

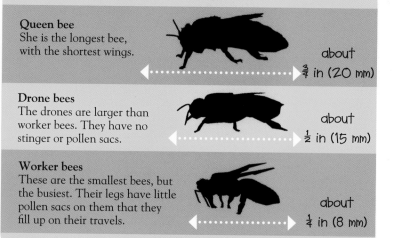

**Queen bee**
She is the longest bee, with the shortest wings.
about ¾ in (20 mm)

**Drone bees**
The drones are larger than worker bees. They have no stinger or pollen sacs.
about ½ in (15 mm)

**Worker bees**
These are the smallest bees, but the busiest. Their legs have little pollen sacs on them that they fill up on their travels.
about ¼ in (8 mm)

Honeycomb is made by bees out of wax they make in their "wax glands". The cells are for storing honey and raising grubs.

## 1. Queen
The queen bee is the mother of all the bees in the colony. There is only one queen bee. She is the only one to lay eggs, which she does in fantastic numbers—as many as 2,000 eggs per day. A good queen lays eggs neatly, one egg to one cell.

## Bee society
Honeybees are sociable creatures and live in highly organized colonies. There are three types of bee. They all undergo "complete metamorphosis" to reach their adult state, changing from egg, to larva, to pupa, to adult.

## 2. Drones
Drones are all male bees. Their only task is to fertilize the queen's eggs and they die in the process. Drones are banished from the hive before winter.

## 3. Workers
These are the bees you see visiting flowers. As their name suggests, they do all the work. They are all female. There are usually many thousand workers (around 60,000+ bees) in a hive during high summer, when pollen and nectar are easily available. This number goes down to about 6,000 over the winter.

larvae in cells

honey store

## "To do"
List of chores for worker bees:

- Feed each larva with honey and pollen for six days.
- On day six, don't forget to seal up each larva's cell, so it can become a pupa.
- Produce more wax and make more honeycomb with it.
- Clean and repair cells.
- Hot weather's coming so beat wings more to ventilate the hive.
- Make honey and check stores.
- Feed and groom the queen (80 times a day!).
- Feed the drones and each other.
- Field bees must go out, gather nectar, pollen, and water, and bring it back for us all to eat and drink.

Bees are **deaf** to most sounds and **mute**. They **communicate** by **vibration** and **smell**.

## How do bees make honey?

Bees use their long tongues to suck nectar into their "honey stomachs." Back at the hive, other worker bees take the nectar from them and "chew" it for about half an hour. The bees then store the chewed nectar in cells, where water evaporates from it, making it thicker. When it is just right, the bees seal the cells with a wax plug.

Bees are vital to flowers. Pollen sticks to their hairy bodies and is transferred to other flowers. This pollinates (or "fertilizes") a flower's seeds.

**DID YOU KNOW?**
Honey collecting by humans is an ancient activity. Cave drawings in Spain dating to 7,000 BCE show figures gathering honey.

Honey is **25%** sweeter than table **sugar.**

Bees collect nectar from flowers and take it to the hive.

## AT A GLANCE
### honey
>>

**DID YOU KNOW?**

In a single trip, a bee will visit between 50 and 100 flowers.

roof

boxes

frames

bees go in here

hive

START HERE

**1** **Busy bees** Making honey starts with the bees. Worker bees collect nectar from flowers and take it back to the hive where they turn the nectar into honey and store it.

**2** **Bees sting!** The beekeeper needs to wear protective clothing. She wears a bee suit, bee gloves, and a bee veil.

**6** **Collecting honey** After the bees have spent a busy summer collecting nectar, it's time to collect the honey. She uses a bee smoker, which calms the bees as she removes the frames.

**7** **Full up!** Here is a frame fresh from the hive. You can see the honey inside the combs. The bees can be gently brushed off with a bee brush.

Honey lasts **forever**—or nearly! **Explorers,** who found some **2,000**-year-old honey, said it tasted **delicious!**

Here the bees make **honey.**

honeycomb

**People** collect the **honey**

and put in jars **ready to eat**

**3 Lots of hives** A beekeeper may have many hives. They must be regularly checked throughout the year.

**4 In winter** Bees need to be fed with honey and sugar water if they are to survive the cold, flower-free months.

**5 In spring** With the budding of spring flowers, bees start to get busy! The beekeeper needs to add extra frames to the hive to store their honey in. Here she is making a frame.

**8 Extracting the honey** The beekeeper places the frames into a honey extracting machine. This machine can hold 12 frames.

**PRODUCTION TIME**

**TO FILL ONE FRAME WITH HONEY:
2–3 WEEKS**

THE END

**9 The final product** Honey! Thanks to the bees' hard work, the beekeeper can now sell the honey, and enjoy it herself!

**DID YOU KNOW?**
One worker bee lives for only a month and produces ½ teaspoon of honey in that time.

# Cotton T-shirt

**During World War II**, T-shirts were standard-issue underwear for soldiers and sailors. They kept the men warm in cold weather, and in hot climates could be worn without a shirt on top. Then people began to see famous actors wearing T-shirts in the movies, and they have been popular fashion items ever since.

cotton boll or seedpod

### What are they made of?

The majority of T-shirts are made of 100 percent cotton. Socks, underwear, shirts, jeans, baby clothes, diapers, and bed linen also contain cotton fiber.

## Uses of cotton

**Fabric**
Cotton is used to make fabric including towels. The material absorbs water well—perfect for bath time.

**Paper**
High-quality paper including US dollar bills are partly made from cotton.

**Explosives**
If cotton is covered with an acid mixture, it explodes when it dries. This material, called guncotton, is similar to gunpowder.

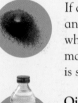
**Oil**
Cotton seeds are made into margarine and oils used in cooking and salad dressings.

**Cotton crops**
Cotton plants can grow up to 10 ft (3 m) high. The seeds are found in the white, fluffy seedpods, called bolls. Each cotton seed is covered with fibers called lint, which are used to make fabric.

## Harvesting cotton

**See how I grow** Cotton plants need plenty of sunshine and water to grow.

**Ready to pick** Warm, dry weather is perfect for harvesting. This farmer is inspecting the crop before it is picked.

**Picking** Cotton is hand picked in poorer countries, but in richer countries a cotton-picker machine like this is used.

**At the gin** The seed and fiber from cotton is divided at a factory called a "gin."

The first paper in China was made of cotton.

DID YOU KNOW?

One cotton plant can produce up to 75 bolls.

**Harvesting** Cotton grown in the US, Australia, and Europe is harvested mechanically. Cotton-picker machines remove the bolls without damaging the plants.

see how it's made

>>

Cotton crops were first grown in Asia and South America over 5,000 years ago..

i ♥ T-shirts

AT A GLANCE
T-shirt
>>

Cotton bolls are picked and spun into cotton yarn.

START HERE

**1 Knitting machine** Fabric is made inside this circular knitting machine. Giant cotton spools threaded through the machine unwind as the fabric is made.

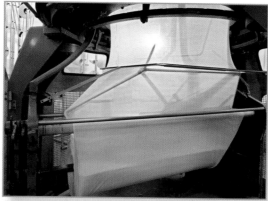

**2 Fabric tube** Inside the machine are over 2,500 needles. These pull and twist the yarn together to make a circular tube of fabric up to 5 ft (1.5 m) across. The fabric is rolled up.

**3 Add color** The fabric is put in a dye machine and chemicals and water are added. The fabric is jiggled around for several hours, then pulled out and passed through a mangle to get rid of excess liquid.

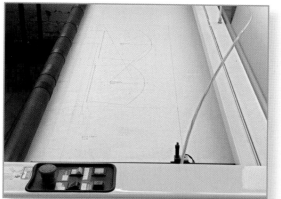

**7 Drawing on the pattern** A digital plotter draws the pattern of the T-shirt on paper. Here you can see all the pieces that fit together to make the finished top.

**8 Cutting out the T-shirt** Next, a worker puts the paper pattern on the fabric and cuts through several layers of fabric at a time, using a sharp electric knife.

**9 Stitching the sleeves and body** The sleeves are hemmed. The body of the T-shirt is stitched together and the sleeves attached. The bottom of the T-shirt is then hemmed.

T-shirts get their name...

The fabric is dyed, cut, and **sewn**

**DID YOU KNOW?** T-shirts are named according to their style and cut. There are tank tops, muscle shirts, scoop necks, V-necks, and lots more!

The **yarn** is knitted into fabric.

to make a **T-shirt**.

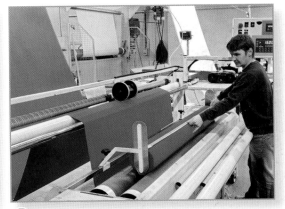

**4** **Cutting open the tube** The fabric tube is slit down one side to make a long single-layer piece of cloth.

**5** **Steam dry** The fabric is then dried, ready to be made into a T-shirt.

**6** **Big blue roll** Next it is measured and rolled up ready to be cut to shape.

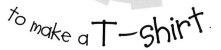
**PRODUCTION TIME**
**FROM COTTON REELS TO T-SHIRT: ABOUT 9 ½ HOURS**

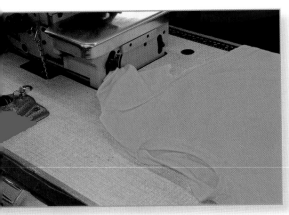

THE END

**10** **Finishing off** The neck is stitched and the T-shirt is finished and ready to be packed and sent to be sold.

**11** **In the store** The T-shirt is ready to be tried on and bought by a customer who likes the color and fit.

**DID YOU KNOW?** In September 2006, American Matt McAllister set a record for wearing the most T-shirts. Dressed in a whopping 155 garments, he had to be cut out with scissors.

...from the **shape** they make when they are **laid out flat**.

# Chocolate

**DID YOU KNOW?**
Over 1,000 years ago, the Maya Indians from Central America used cocoa beans as their currency.

**The making of chocolate** begins in the hot and humid tropical rain forests where cacao trees grow. Throughout the year, small flowers blossom on the trunks and main branches of the trees. About 30 flowers on each tree become huge golden-red pods, the size of pineapples. Break one of these pods open and inside you'll find 30 to 40 seeds. These are cocoa beans—the key part of chocolate.

cacao blossoms

The cocoa pods take four to five months to ripen.

The cocoa beans are surrounded by sticky white pulp.

52 The Mayans also used cocoa beans to make a drink called chocolatl.

# Preparing the beans

dried cocoa beans

The farmers prepare the beans by hand, as they have for over a thousand years.

### Scooping out the beans
The farmers scoop out the wet cocoa beans from the pods. They spread them on banana leaves, cover, and then leave them to ferment for about a week. This removes the beans' bitter taste and allows the all-important chocolate flavor to develop.

### Sun-dried beans
The fermented beans are now spread out in the sun and left to dry. Once dry, the farmers bag them up and ship them to a factory. There, the beans are poured into huge roasting drums. Then they're transferred to a hulling machine, where the shells are removed, leaving the insides of the beans, called the nibs.

cocoa mass

The cocoa mass is pure, unsweetened chocolate and much too bitter to eat.

Together cocoa mass and cocoa butter are called cocoa solids. The percentage of cocoa solids used in making a chocolate bar is shown on its label.

cocoa butter

### Squeeeeeze!
The nibs are ground down to make a thick paste. This is then pressed to separate the cocoa butter from the cocoa mass. The cocoa mass is poured into moulds and left to cool and solidify. This is now ready to be made into chocolate bars and treats.

The cocoa butter is the fatty substance in cocoa beans.

see how it's made

>>

Cocoa beans are made up of about half cocoa butter and half cocoa mass.

Ground cocoa beans are made into **cocoa mass.**

ground cocoa beans

Add **sugar**

plus powdered **full-fat milk**

**START HERE**

**1** **Breaking up** First, a worker has to break up the solid block of cocoa mass (the pure chocolate found in cocoa beans) using a knife.

**2** **All systems go!** The cocoa mass is put into the chocolate-making machine, which gently warms, turns, and massages the ingredients.

**6** **In goes the cocoa butter** The worker adds cocoa butter (the fatty substance found in cocoa beans). The machine melts and stirs the cocoa butter into the chocolate, making it runny.

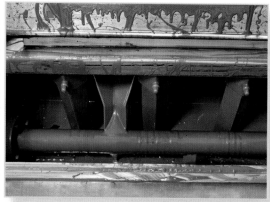

**7** **Milling process** The runny chocolate is then forced through pipes and over ball bearings. To make sure the mix becomes very smooth, this milling process continues for six hours.

**8** **Tempering process** The chocolate is heated slowly, then poured into a shallow container, where it is stirred gently to spread the cocoa butter evenly as the chocolate is slowly cooled.

The United States of America produces the most chocolate...

...and cocoa butter.

Mill them to make them smooth

for yummy chocolate treats.

DID YOU KNOW?
White chocolate contains no cocoa mass. That's why some people say it's not "real" chocolate.

**3** **In goes the sugar** The worker adds sugar to the cocoa mass in the machine.

**4** **In goes the milk** Powdered full-fat milk is poured into the machine, too. The machine begins gently to shake, stir, and mix the ingredients.

**5** **Dry conching process** For 48 hours, the machine aerates (adds air to) the mix, allowing the rich smell and flavor to develop. The ingredients form a thick paste.

**9** **Into the molds** The chocolate is then poured into molds by a machine. These molds can be all shapes and sizes. Some machines can fill more than 1,000 molds in a minute.

**10** **Hardening up** The molds are placed in a huge fridge where the chocolate cools and hardens.

PRODUCTION TIME
FROM MELTING TO REMOVING THE MOLDS: ABOUT 3 DAYS

**11** **They're ready** The worker removes the chocolate treats from their molds. The chocolates are wrapped and boxed ready to be taken to stores.

THE END

...but the Swiss eat the most chocolate per person.

# Pencils

**People have been writing** with pencils for centuries. Did you ever wonder how they were invented? Or what they're made from? Or how the writing part gets into the middle?

graphite + clay

**Graphite chunks** are ground into coarse grains.

**Special clay** is combined with the ground graphite.

## The birth of the pencil...

**About 1500, shepherds noticed hard black lumps around the roots of a fallen tree in Cumberland, England.**

At first they thought it was coal, but it wouldn't burn. Later, they found it was great for marking sheep—soon they were making pencils.

This makes a breadcrumby substance called pellet mix.

The more graphite that's mixed with the clay, the softer, or smudgier, a pencil will be.

*Baaaa*

The first pencils were pieces of graphite wrapped up in **sheepskin.**

*Baaaa*

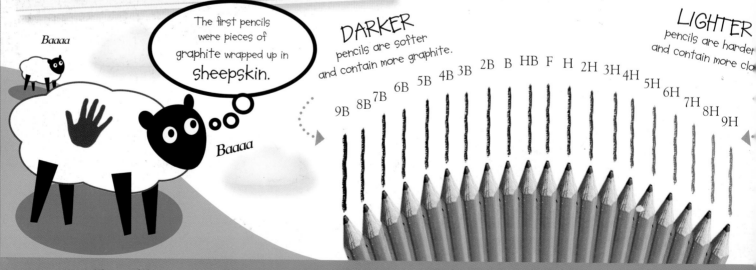

DARKER pencils are softer and contain more graphite.

LIGHTER pencils are harder and contain more cla...

9B 8B 7B 6B 5B 4B 3B 2B B HB F H 2H 3H 4H 5H 6H 7H 8H 9H

Pencil **"lead"** is not lead at all—it's **graphite,** which is mined from the ground.

Pellet mix goes into a tube where it's squashed into a hard cylinder called a billet.

The billet is forced through a hole to make thin strips, which are cut into pencil lengths.

**DID YOU KNOW?**
A new pencil has enough graphite in it to draw a line almost 35 miles (56 km) long.

The pencil lengths are dusted with chalk so they don't stick together, then spun in a machine (main picture) to remove moisture. Finally, they get fired in an oven and soaked in wax before they are ready to go into pencils.

see how it's made

>>

The outside of pencils is made from cedar wood, which is ideal because it has hardly any knots in it.

Grooves are cut in each slat,

then graphite strips are glued in the grooves.

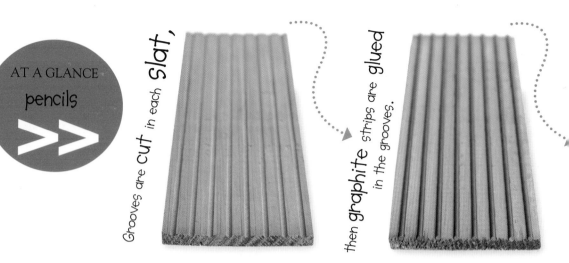

Thin rectangles of cedar, called "slats," are cut from solid wood that has been soaked in wax. Grooves are cut into the slats.

START HERE

**1** **Sticky solution** A tiny row of nozzles squeezes exactly the right amount of glue along the length of each groove, ready to receive the graphite core.

**2** **Core positioning** A large roller drops the graphite strips into the glued grooves of half the batch of prepared cedar slats.

**6** **Nearly there** The pencils are pushed out of the cutting-and-shaping machine and dropped into a large container, ready for the next stage.

**7** **Shiny finish** The bare wooden pencils are passed through a bath of paint or lacquer, then dried, then passed through the bath again. This gives them a protective finish.

**8** **Right to the point** Finally, rows of painted pencils are sharpened all together on a huge rotating sandpaper belt.

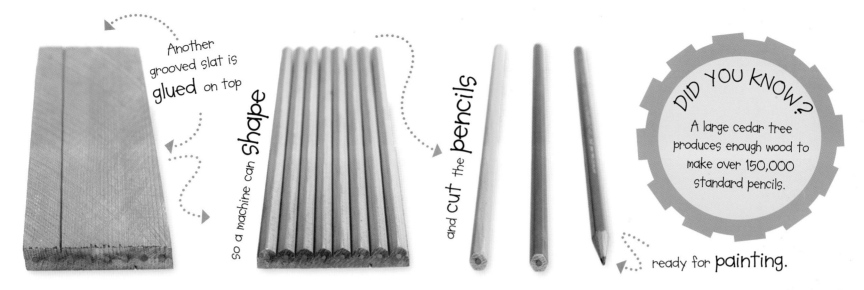

Another grooved slat is **glued** on top

So a machine can **shape**

and **cut** the **pencils**

ready for **painting**.

DID YOU KNOW?

A large cedar tree produces enough wood to make over 150,000 standard pencils.

**3 Making a sandwich** The rest of the grooved, glued slats are placed directly on the filled slats, forming what looks like pencil "sandwiches."

**4 Time and pressure** All the sandwiches are clamped tightly together and left overnight so the glue inside them can harden.

**5 Shaping and separating** They then go into a machine that separates the pencils and cuts them into shape—round or hexagonal (with six flat sides).

**9 Final touch** The sharpened pencils are ready for one more stage—a quick dip in contrasting paint to add banding at one end.

PRODUCTION TIME
FROM WOOD SLATS TO PENCILS: ABOUT 5 DAYS

**10 On their way** The finished pencils are placed by hand in tin boxes, packed in cartons, and delivered to stores all over the world.

THE END

Most pencils have several coats of paint or lacquer on the outside.

The world's **largest pencil** is 65 ft (19 m) **long**—it took two years to make.

# Electric guitar

**People have played string instruments for thousands of years,** but the guitar as we know it wasn't developed until the 16th century. It was during the 1930s, though, that electric guitars first appeared—since then they have dominated the worlds of jazz, blues, pop, and rock music.

**Plucking choice**
Guitar strings are plucked with a plectrum (left), or a pick that fits over the thumb (right).

Bridge where strings are attached

Electrical pickups

Solid wood body

Electric guitars usually have six strings that are plucked with the fingertips or strummed with a pick or plectrum.

**DID YOU KNOW?**
During a 1964 US tour, George Harrison of The Beatles was given a 12-string guitar, which he used from then on.

Tone and volume controls

Cutaway allows fingers to reach high frets.

The famous rock guitarist Jimi Hendrix was left handed, so he played a right-handed guitar upside down.

## Acoustic guitars

Traditional guitars have a hollow body. The sound made when you pluck the strings bounces off the wood and echoes through the space to make it louder and richer.

## Electric guitars work like this...

1. When the strings are plucked, they vibrate.

2. The vibration is caught by a pickup that converts it into electrical signals.

3. These electrical signals are sent to an amplifier that boosts the signals.

4. The boosted signals are sent to a loudspeaker that converts them into sound we can hear.

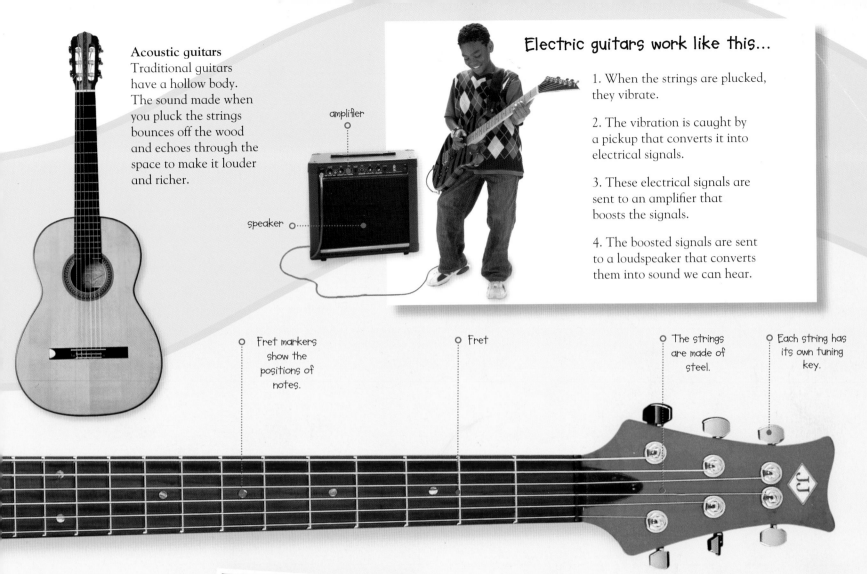

amplifier

speaker

Fret markers show the positions of notes.

Fret

The strings are made of steel.

Each string has its own tuning key.

## Big notes

Outside the Hard Rock Cafe at Universal City Studios in Hollywood sits a giant 78 ft (24 m) neon green electric guitar in the shape of a Fender Stratocaster, one of the most famous models ever produced.

## Neck and neck

On the whole guitars, like people, have only one neck, but they can have two, or three, or more. Here, Rick Neilson of Cheap Trick plays a custom-made five-neck instrument.

The Fender Stratocaster electric guitar, first available in 1954, is still a best seller today.

Sheets of **wood** are glued **together.** ⋯⋯> The body **shape** is cut out and holes are **drilled** for the electric cables. ⋯⋯

START HERE

**1** **Raw material**. Guitar bodies are usually made from mahogany, alder, or ash. The maker begins by choosing his material from the long pieces of wood stored in the workshop.

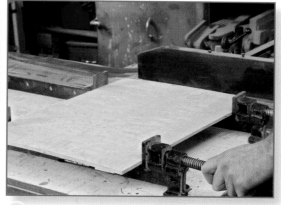

**2** **Slicing and gluing** A piece of maple that will go on the front of the guitar is formed by glueing two sheets together, edge-to-edge.

**3** **On the surface** The maple is glued onto the wood selected for the guitar body. The finished piece is pushed through a sanding machine to make it smooth.

**7** **Neck details** A strip of rosewood—the fingerboard—covers the truss rod. With this in place, the maker drills pegholes in the top of the neck and shapes its bottom to fit the guitar body.

**8** **Attaching the frets** Then he cuts a row of straight grooves across the fingerboard and hammers a length of fret wire into each one.

**9** **Putting it all together** The neck's shaped bottom is carefully slotted into the corresponding hollow in the instrument's body.

Twelve-string guitars have six double rows of strings.

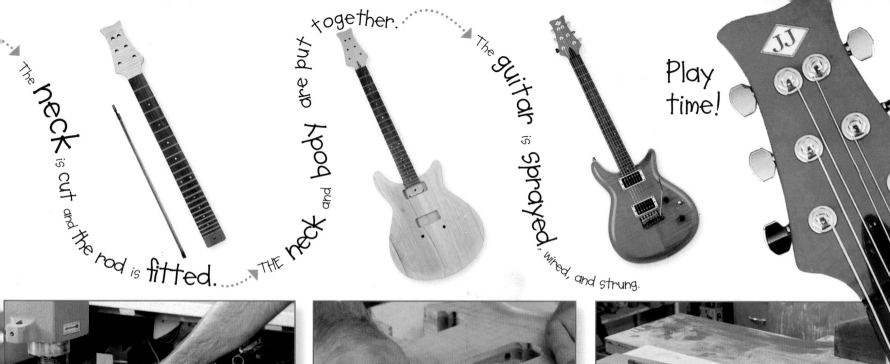

The **neck** is cut and the rod is **fitted**. ⟶ THE **neck** and **body** are put together. ⟶ The **guitar** is **sprayed**, wired, and strung.

**Play time!**

**4  Cutting the wood** The maker uses a wooden template to cut out the guitar shape with an electric saw called a router. This tool also cuts holes for the electric cables.

**5  Cover that edge** A strip of flexible plastic is stuck down to neaten the edge. This is smoothed into place with a special tool called a thumb plane.

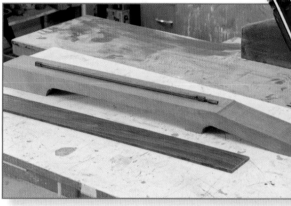

**6  Forming the neck** The maker's next job is to cut out the neck of the guitar with his router. To strengthen it, he inserts a metal truss rod into a groove he's made along the length.

**10  Bright and shiny** The maker fits all the necessary electrical parts and wires. He sprays the guitar body with paint and lacquer and polishes it to make it shiny.

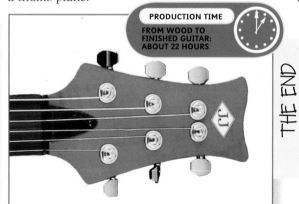

**PRODUCTION TIME**
**FROM WOOD TO FINISHED GUITAR: ABOUT 22 HOURS**

**11  All strung out** The strings are attached and anchored around the keys so they can be loosened or tightened. Now the guitar is ready to play.

**THE END**

**DID YOU KNOW?** If you're in the audience at a rock concert, the sound is as loud as a chain saw held in your hands.

Legendary guitarists **Eric Clapton** and **Hank Marvin** have electric guitars **named** after them.

63

# Ceramic mug

**People have been mining clay** and making it into pots for thousands of years. Clay is an ideal material for this purpose because it's easy to work with, and once it's heated to high temperatures, it becomes strong and hard and able to hold its shape. The finished pieces are described as ceramic. People still make pots by hand, but factory methods are best for turning out lots of bowls, plates, cups, and mugs of the same shape and size.

Clay is found in huge clay pits like this one, photographed from the air.

china clay

## Clay

Clay is a kind of fine soil. When it's wet it's easy to mold, and when it's dry it holds its shape—when it's fired, it holds its shape for centuries. Clay can be whitish, buff, brown, green, olive, or blue. The purest clay, called china clay, is used to make a strong, smooth material called porcelain—it's so thin, you can see light through it.

**By hand**
Potters start with a lump of clay. They wet it on the outside so they can shape it easily.

Sometimes potters use ropes or sheets of clay to make pots.

pot made in 2200 BCE

**Magic wheel**
Handmade pottery is often shaped on a potters' wheel. The potter places a ball of clay on the wheel and gently raises the clay as it turns to form a hollow shape. Wheels are powered with either a foot pedal or a motor.

## Types of ceramic:

**Earthenware**
Pottery made from fairly coarse clay and fired at low temperatures. Earthenware is thicker than porcelain.

**Stoneware**
A dense, thick, nonabsorbent pottery that is fired at very high temperatures.

**Bone china**
A type of porcelain that gets its name from the fact that burned animal bones are mixed with the clay to make it especially fine, thin, strong, and white.

Clay that has so much **water** added that it's almost **liquid** is called **"slip."**

**DID YOU KNOW?** Fine pottery is called china because porcelain was first imported to Europe from China during the 16th century.

see how it's made

**>>**

Slip is mostly used for the **body** of a piece of pottery, and sometimes for **decoration**.

A handful of **clay**

goes into the **mold**

and out comes

a **perfect** mug shape

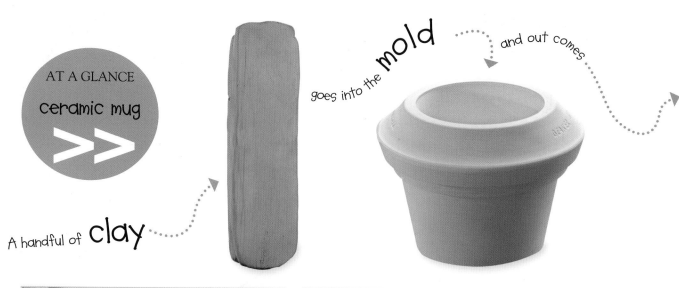

**1** **Start with the clay** First the potter grabs a handful of clay. From long practice, he is able to pick up exactly the right amount to make one mug.

**2** **Into the mold** He throws the clay into a mold. An automatic shaping tool presses down inside to spread it. Then the mold spins around very fast, shaping the clay into a mug shape.

**3** **Out of the mold** Next the potter puts the mold, with the clay mug inside, into a special room where the clay begins to dry. When it is no longer sticky, the potter lifts the mug out.

**7** **Into the oven** When the mug is dry, it is ready to be baked, or "fired," for the first time. Inside a big oven called a kiln, mugs, bowls, and vases are all fired together on racks.

**8** **Printed pattern** To make the colored transfer that will decorate the mug, the pattern is printed on large sheets of tissue paper and hung on lines where they're easy to reach.

**9** **Cut it out** Once the mug has cooled down from its first firing, a skilled worker cuts off pieces of tissue paper and wraps them around the body and the handle.

**Pottery** that has been fired in a **kiln** only once is called **biscuit ware.**

On goes the **handle** then the mug is fired in the **kiln.**

A pretty **pattern** is stuck on and the mug is **fired** again.

Finally, it's **dipped in glaze** and fired for the **third and last** time.

**DID YOU KNOW?** In the kiln, the temperature reaches more than 1,800°F (1,000°C)— about four times hotter than a kitchen oven.

It's time for **coffee!**

**4 Off to storage** Sometimes, these half-made mugs (they have no handles) are put aside to wait for the next stage.

**5 Waiting room** Here, hundreds and hundreds of mug shapes are stacked up to the ceiling until they're needed.

**6 Handle on** When it's time, the potter sticks the handle to the mug using slip. A sponge is perfect for removing any drips.

**10 Stick it on** A special liquid soap is brushed on over the colored pattern to make it stick to the mug. When the pattern is in place, the excess tissue paper is washed away.

**11 A quick dip** Next the mug is fired for a second time, then dipped in a liquid glaze that seals the pattern and makes the surface shiny. When it's fired, the glaze is clear.

**PRODUCTION TIME**
FROM LUMP OF CLAY TO FINISHED MUG: ABOUT 36 HOURS

**12 Fired again** Now the mug is fired for the third, and last, time. Once it has cooled down, it's ready to be packed up carefully and shipped to a store.

THE END

The **earliest existing** ceramic figure is **27,000** years old.

Manila hemp plant

This plant has huge green leaves, about 6 ft (2 m) long. These contain fibers that are stripped out and twisted into rope.

# Rope

**Rope is made by twisting fibers** together to create long, strong twine for tying and pulling things. Humans have worked with rope since before records began, but among early rope users were the ancient Egyptians.

The ancient Egyptians used rope to pull things, such as the boat in this picture, or the huge rocks they used to build their pyramids.

manila hemp rope

Originally rope was made from **animal hair, leather,** or reeds. But today we use

man-made rope

Nylon is an oil-based synthetic fiber that makes strong and elastic rope.

**The rope walk**
Traditionally, rope is made in a very long building called a rope walk.

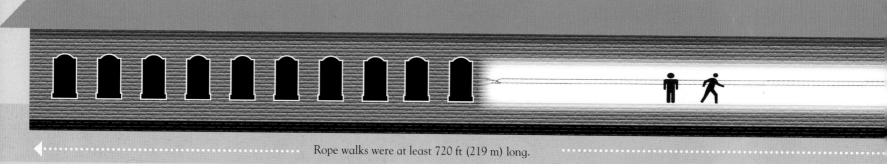

Rope walks were at least 720 ft (219 m) long.

The **coarse fiber** around **coconut shells** is called **coir**.

### Rope rigging

Manila hemp rope was used to rig old sailing ships such as British commander Nelson's *HMS Captain*. Larger sailing ships used around 30 miles (48 km) of rope each to secure the masts, operate the sails, and steer the ship.

In 1797, rigged sailing ships fought the Battle of Cape St. Vincent between the British and Spanish fleets. The British won.

### Modern rope

As rope-making materials improve, manufacturers are able to reduce the thickness of rope without losing strength. Sometimes rope is made from iron or steel wires. Called cable, this is used to pull up elevators or support bridges.

In helicopter rescue, ropes are used with winches to lift stranded people to safety.

either **natural plant fibers** including manila hemp, or

**man-made** fibers such as **nylon.**

Another man-made fiber – polypropylene – makes lightweight, floating rope used to section off lanes in swimming pools.

Polyester, also man made, makes a tough, hard-wearing rope often used on boats.

The room was called a rope walk because at one time a worker had to walk the length of the room as he twisted the rope by hand.

**Coir** is used to make **hairy brown rope** and floor coverings.

Start with a **plant** called **manila hemp.**

Scrape **fibers** from the **leaves.**

**START HERE**

**1** **The raw material** This is manila hemp, a natural fiber widely used for rope. It looks and feels like thick, coarse, matted hair.

**2** **Untangle time** The chosen rope fibers are fed into a machine that starts to untangle them. A cone-shaped tool spirals them into a neat pile when they come out of the machine.

**3** **Combing the fiber** The fibers are dragged across metal pins, like rows of giant combs, so all the fibers face the same direction. At the same time, the fibers are sprayed to stop from them rotting.

**7** **Twisting yarn into strands** Yarn from the bobbins is fed through part of the machine that looks a bit like a colander. The yarn is twisted together to make thicker strands.

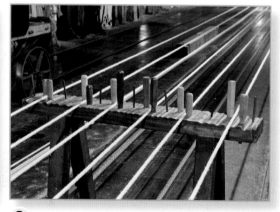

**8** **Positioning the strands** Here, the strands are laid out ready for twisting. Six strands will make two lengths of rope.

**9** **Anchoring to the hooks** At the other end of the factory, the strands are attached to hooks on a machine that will twist them into rope.

**Rope** sold to the **Royal Navy** is measured in **fathoms,** which are used to measure the **depth of water.**

Spin fibers into **yarn**.

Twist **yarn** into strands.

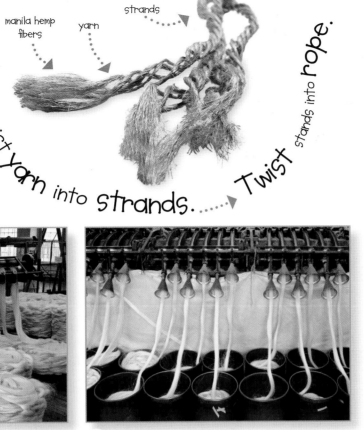

manila hemp fibers

yarn

strands

rope

Twist strands into **rope**.

DID YOU KNOW?

Manilla rope doesn't soak up sea water so it's often used on boats.

**4** **Making loose strands** The fibers are drawn together to make several long, loose, continuous strands.

**5** **More combing** The fibers pass through three combing machines until they are the same thickness and weight along their length. Then they are coiled into buckets.

**6** **Twisting yarn** Next they are threaded onto a machine, called a flier, where they are spun into yarn and wound onto big bobbins.

PRODUCTION TIME
FROM YARN TO FINISHED ROPE: UP TO 2 HOURS

THE END

**10** **Twisting rope** The hooks twist the strands together three at a time. As they twist, they tighten and become shorter.

**11** **Collecting the rope** When the rope is fully twisted, it is wound onto a huge reel for easy storage.

**12** **Sealing the ends** The ends of the rope will unravel if they are left, so they are tied or sealed with black tape until the rope is ready for use.

A fathom was **originally** the **width** of a man's **outstretched arms.**

**1,128 FEET LENGTH**
**47 ½ " " BREADTH**

>>

How long is a piece of rope? At one time rope was as long as the room in which it was made. This is because the strands were attached to hooks at either end of the room, then twisted together into rope.

Here rope is made along the whole length of the factory—that's a leg-aching ¼ mile (400 m). Workers use a bicycle to get from one end of the factory to the other.

A big rope buyer, the British Navy required rope to be a minimum length of 120 fathoms (720 ft/219 m

**Admiral Lord Nelson,** the British naval commander who won the famous battle of Trafalgar, bought rope at this factory. He walked the rope walk in this photograph.

That's about the length of two football fields, so the rope walk had to be at least this long.

# Cheese

**Legend has it that** the first cheese was made by accident over 4,000 years ago. Traveling goat herders carried milk in a bag made from a goat's stomach. A substance in the stomach (called rennet), together with warm weather and a bumpy ride, made the milk separate into a watery liquid and a soft cheesy solid. From this modest beginning, cheese making has become big business, with over 1,000 different varieties produced each year.

**Holey cheese**
Bacteria in Swiss cheese make a gas that bubbles up through the cheese leaving holes.

**Tasty treats**
Cheese can be eaten on its own, in savory dishes, and in yummy desserts, such as this lemon cheesecake.

emmenthal

feta

camember

mascarpone

buffalo mozzarella

cottage cheese

edam

brie

gruyèr

**Blue veins**
The blue veins in blue cheese are made from edible fungus.

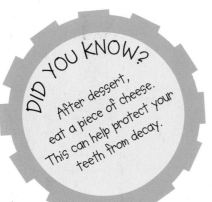

## DID YOU KNOW?

After dessert, eat a piece of cheese. This can help protect your teeth from decay.

## All kinds of cheese

Most commonly, cheese is made from cows' milk. But it can also be made from the milk of other animals including yak, camel, reindeer, horse, sheep, goat, and buffalo.

yak

camel

reindeer

horse

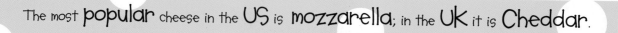

The most **popular** cheese in the US is **mozzarella**; in the UK it is **Cheddar**.

**DID YOU KNOW?**
It takes about 21 pts (10 liters) of milk to make 2 lbs (1 kg) of Cheddar cheese.

goat's cheese

roquefort

monterey jack

parmesan

goat's cheese

sheep

goat

buffalo

**In the storeroom** cheese is kept at 50°F (10°C). The cheese takes at least 14 months to mature before it is eaten.

see how it's made
>>

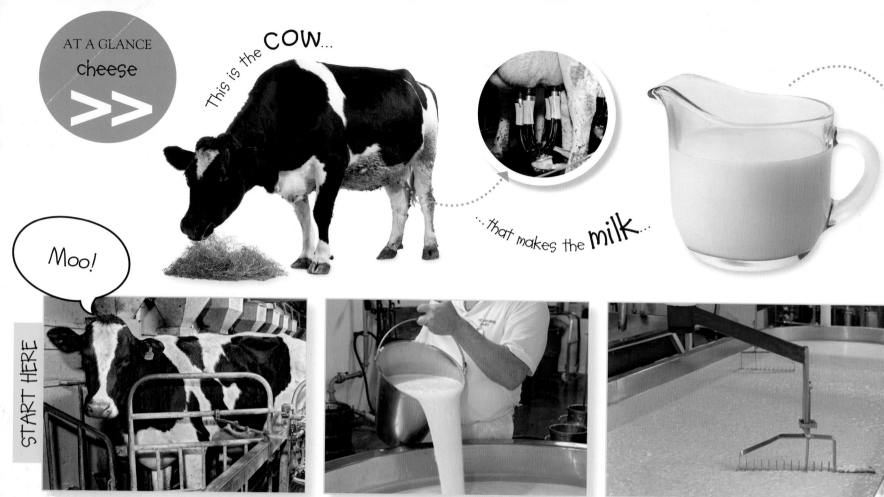

This is the COW...

Moo!

...that makes the milk...

START HERE

**1** **On the farm** Cows are milked on farms close to the dairy, which means the milk is really fresh.

**2** **At the dairy** A starter culture is added to the milk. It is stirred and slowly warmed to around 95°F (35°C).

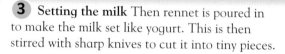

**3** **Setting the milk** Then rennet is poured in to make the milk set like yogurt. This is then stirred with sharp knives to cut it into tiny pieces.

**7** **Milling and salting** The springy curds are then put through a metal mill where they are chopped. The cheesemakers sprinkle salt from a bucket over the curds.

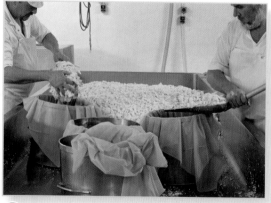

**8** **Pressed into molds** The milled curds are packed into round molds lined with cloth. The molds are put into a cheese press that squeezes out any remaining moisture.

**9** **Wrapped and greased** After the cheese has been pressed for 24 hours, it is lifted out of its mold, wrapped in a soft cheesecloth bandage, greased with lard, and pressed again.

On average one COW produces 34–42 pints (16–20 liters) of milk a day...

...that's turned into **curds**...

...that are put in a **mold**...

...and matures into **cheese**...

...that we **eat**.

**DID YOU KNOW?**
The whey that's drained from milk in the cheesemaking process is fed to animals such as pigs.

**4** **Curds and whey** The tiny pieces are called curds. The liquid is called whey.

**5** **Drain and cool** The whey is drained off and the curd, which will become the cheese, is transferred into a slightly sloping cooling tray where the moisture drains away.

**6** **"Cheddaring"** Cheesemakers cut, stack, and repeatedly turn the curd to make sure all the moisture drains away. This is called "cheddaring."

**PRODUCTION TIME**

FROM MILK TO CHEESE: ABOUT 14 MONTHS

**10** **Stored and turned** The cheese is lifted out of the mold and taken to the store room where it is turned over regularly as it matures. The room is kept cool, but humid.

**11** **Finally ready** The cheese is checked during the maturing process to make sure the color, taste, smell, and texture are just right. After 14 months it ready to be unwrapped.

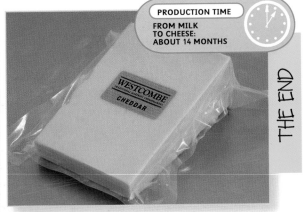

**12** **Ready for the store** Then it's cut into smaller pieces and packed to keep it fresh. The cheese is finally packed into boxes and sent to stores for sale.

THE END

...that's **enough** to make about **4 lbs (2 kg)** of cheese.

# Soap

**Lavender soap, oatmeal soap, soap shaped like a heart...** There are hundreds of soaps available in the stores, but they are all made from the same basic ingredients: oil and caustic soda. Together these loosen dirt and grease so they can be washed away with water.

soapstone

### Is it soap?
Although this soft rock feels like soap it is mostly made from the mineral talc, which is used to make talcum powder as well as paints and pottery. Soapstone is a popular material for sculpting since it can be cut easily with a knife.

### Soap work
Among the early soap makers were the Romans, who made soap from goat fat and wood ash. They used soap to clean their clothes.

*mmm...goat fat and ash for a nice clean toga.*

*Rich Romans would bathe in wine and the women sometimes bathed in milk.*

### Soap plant
When you boil the soapwort plant in water it produces soap that is gentle enough to clean damaged hair, sensitive skin, and delicate fabric. Soapwort is also known as Bouncing Bet, Wild Sweet William, and Farewell Summer.

### Scrape clean
To clean themselves, the early Greeks rubbed their bodies with clay, sand, and oil. They used a metal tool called a *strigil* to scrape off the clay, sand, oil, and dirt from their skin.

People **first made** soap around **5,000** years ago.

**Soap noodles** are a common ingredient in soap bars today. These are made when oil and an alkali, such as caustic soda, are mixed, heated, and dried. This results in soft soap that is fed into a machine and cut into noodles. Perfume and color are added to soap noodles to make bars of soap.

**The soap factory** has a mixing room where technicians make samples of soap before production can begin.

DID YOU KNOW?
TV dramas about people's everyday lives are called soap operas because they were originally paid for by US soap manufacturers.

Fragrant oils are tested to find the best scent.

Colors are tried to see which one looks best.

see how it's made

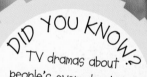

Start with **soap** NOODLES!

Add **smell** and **color**.

Jiggle the mix together...

START HERE

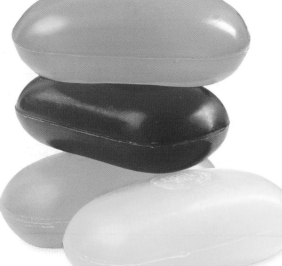

**1** **Sample soaps** Technicians make sample soaps to try out different quantities of perfume and color. Once they get this right, lots of bars of soap can be made.

**2** **Making soap for sale** First the color and perfume are mixed together. They are then added to the soap noodles and jiggled around until all the noodles are completely coated.

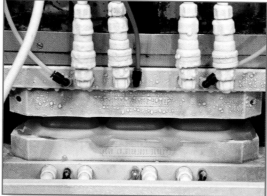

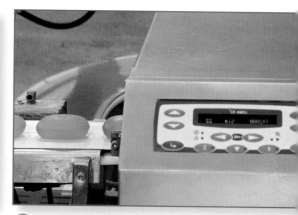

**6** **Cold mold** The billets are laid across a mold in the stamper. The mold is kept very cold since this stops the soap from getting stuck to it.

**7** **Stamping into shape** The top of the mold is lowered down to cut the billet into bars of soap. Leftover pieces of soap are put back into the mixing machine.

**8** **Check for metal** The bars of soap pass through a metal detector. This makes sure pieces of metal—from the machines used during production—haven't gotten into the bars of soap.

**Soap bubbles** are really delicate **spheres**, formed when you rub a bar of **soap** with **water**.

Then squeeze it into a **Solid** piece.

**Cut** the piece into **bars**.

Ready for **bath time.**

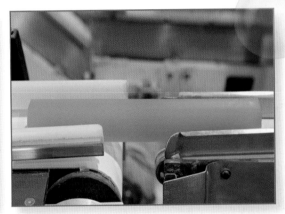

**3** **Blending** The noodles are blended together and pushed through fine mesh in a machine called a refining plodder. The mixture then travels on a conveyor belt to a vacuum plodder machine.

**4** **Bursting bubbles** High pressure in the vacuum plodder is used to suck out any air bubbles from the mixture. The soap then comes out as one solid piece.

**5** **Billets of soap** The soap then gets cut into smaller blocks of soap, called billets. These pass along to the stamper machine.

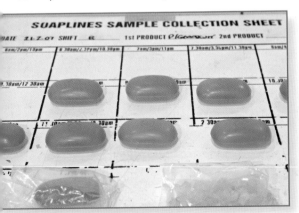

**PRODUCTION TIME**
FROM NOODLES
TO BARS OF SOAP:
ABOUT 20 MINUTES

THE END

**DID YOU KNOW?** The traditional name for a person who makes soap is "soaper." Some people make their own soap at home.

**9** **Quality control** The soap is checked at regular intervals throughout the day to make sure the color, size, and shape are all correct.

**10** **Finished product** Finally, the soap is wrapped and boxed and sent off to the stores to be sold.

During World War II, **secret messages** were hidden inside **soap-bar wrappers.**

# Crayons

**The earliest crayons were made in Europe** from a mixture of oil and charcoal. Later, pigments were added and the oil was replaced with wax. But it wasn't until 1903 that the first wax crayons, made especially for children, went on sale in the US. These were soft, they had flat tips, and they were cheap enough for children to buy.

And here are the dimensions.
Height: 4.5 metres (15 feet)
Weight: 680 kg (1500 lbs)

**Giant size**
This record-breaking crayon was unveiled in October 2003 in Easton, Pennsylvania. It's made from small pieces of worn-down crayons, it's taller than two men, and it weighs more than a cow.

## How wax works

Paraffin wax, which is used in wax crayons, is taken from coal and petroleum. Coal and petroleum are made from dead plants that have been buried for millions of years.

$+$ millions of years later $=$ $+$ $=$

*Crayons are made!*

Plants have a waxy coating. This does not rot away.

Heat and pressure turn the plants into petroleum.

Wax is removed from the petroleum.

Color pigments are added.

**Color ways**
In the first box of eight wax crayons, colors were black, brown, blue, red, violet, orange, yellow, and green. Today, there are hundreds of colors to choose from. Each has its own name including Blue Bell, Vivid Violet, and Electric Lime.

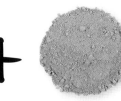

**No smudge!**
Wax crayons are great for children since they hardly smudge at all.

*perfect for coloring*

There are lots of things to **color** with including **glitter pens, fluorescent pens...**

<<

Affordable crayons like these are found in schools and homes around the world. Over three billion of them are made every year.

DID YOU KNOW?

Crayon is the French word for pencil.

See how it's made
>>

...and scented pens that add fragrance as you draw.

powdered pigments

and paraffin wax

START HERE

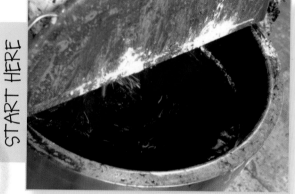

**1** **Melting and mixing** Crayons begin as paraffin wax and colored pigments. The wax is melted in a large container, called a kettle, and mixed with the pigments.

**2** **Pouring** Next the runny wax mixture is poured into a big bucket with a wide pouring lip.

**6** **Labeling** Next, a label is wrapped right around each crayon. The crayons roll into collecting bins.

**7** **Ready for boxing** Cartoned by color, the crayons are lifted onto a big rotating table. Now they are ready to go into their own boxes.

kettle

**mixed** in a kettle and poured into **molds.**

Here they harden into **crayons.**

Then they're put into **boxes.**

DID YOU KNOW?

In the US, the most popular crayon color is blue.

**3 Filling molds** Then it's poured out of the bucket onto a tray of crayon-shaped molds. The mixture fills the molds.

**4 Hardening** It takes a few minutes for the mixture to cool and harden into crayons. The new crayons are lifted out of the molds.

**5 Inspection time!** All the crayons are checked for quality. Any that have holes or pieces missing are remelted and remade.

**8 The sorting machine** Workers choose the colors they need for a particular selection box, and pour them into a collating machine.

**9 One of each color** The collating machine takes one of each color and slips the crayons into boxes ready for stores.

PRODUCTION TIME

FROM MIXING TO BOXING: UP TO 5 DAYS

THE END

...you would need more than **40 million** to go around the **Earth.**

# Glass bottle

**Today, handblown glass** is an expensive luxury, but for around 2,000 years it was the most common kind of glassware available. Then, in 1903, American glassmaker Michael Owens invented a fully automated bottle-blowing machine. This was a giant leap forward. Now, glass bottles for storing foods, drinks, medicines, and much more could be produced quickly and cheaply.

Michael Owen's 10-arm bottle-making machine could produce up to four bottles per minute.

>>

**On average,** families in the UK use more than 300 bottles and glass jars each year. Almost all of these are mass-produced in factories like the one shown here.

## What's good about glass?

**You can see through it**
Much of the glass we see every day is in windows and bottles. We look out of buildings, and into bottles to see if they're full.

**Good insulation**
Glass fiber is made from millions of tiny shreds of glass. It keeps heat in houses and is also used to make boat hulls.

**Heatproof**
Usually known by its trade name, Pyrex, this heat-resistant glass can withstand sudden changes of temperature.

**Fine focus**
Optical glass bends light to focus on the right place at the back of your eye so you can see.

Sort **bottles** and **jars** into **colors** when you recycle.

**These bottles** are leaving a multisection machine and moving on to conveyor belts. This is one of 13 production lines at the factory.

V V

DID YOU KNOW?

A layer of wax is sprayed on bottles to make them virtually unscratchable.

This is a fruit-juice bottle.

## Recycling glass

Glass can be recycled over and over again and every bottle it is made into will be as good as the first. And, since glass melts at lower temperatures than the raw materials it's made from in the first place, recycling glass uses less energy than making it from scratch.

If you recycle just one glass bottle, you will save enough energy to power your TV for 15 minutes.

see how it's made

>>

The **new bottles** will then have **top-quality,** pure **color.**

Ingredients including **sand**, soda ash, limestone, and **recycled glass** are mixed together

recycled glass (called cullet)

sand

soda ash

limestone

**DID YOU KNOW?**

Glass forms naturally when heat from a volcano melts sand. The resulting glassy rock is called obsidian.

START HERE

**1** **Scoop it up!** First the raw ingredients, including sand, soda ash, limestone, and recycled glass, are scooped up and carried to the factory.

**2** **Weigh in** The ingredients are poured through a giant funnel onto scales below, where they are carefully weighed. Then they are carried off on conveyor belts with wire mesh sides.

**6** **Rough bottles** Each gob drops into a mold roughly shaped like a bottle. A plunger presses into the gob forcing it to take the mold's shape. The mold opens and the bottle is lifted out.

**7** **Final shape** Next, molds shaped exactly like the finished bottles are closed around the hot glass. Then the glass is blown and sucked into the final bottle shape.

**8** **Cooling down** Now the bottles pass through a cooling oven, called a lehr. These bottles are coming out of the lehrs.

Mass-produced bottles like these...

Then they're **shaped** and **cooled**...

...they are **melted** in a **furnace**.

ready for **filling!**

**DID YOU KNOW?**
Glass bottles can be any color from pale blue to dark brown. However, the most popular bottles are clear.

**3 Computer control** The factory is controlled by computers. These manage the furnace temperatures and the speed bottles are made and moved through the factory.

**4 Mix and melt** The ingredients are mixed together, then poured into a huge furnace. Heated to 2,732°F (1,500°C), the mix melts to a liquid. This is molten glass. It is so hot that it glows white.

**5 Cutting gobs** The molten glass flows from the furnace along channels. Then it is chopped into lengths, called gobs, each exactly the right size to make one bottle.

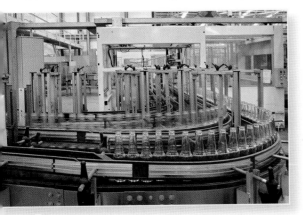

**9 Moving on** The bottles travel around the factory on conveyor belts. These bottles are on their way to be packed.

**10 Quality checks** Bottles are regularly checked and tested for quality. They have to be perfect. Any that don't make the grade are sent back to the furnace for recycling.

**PRODUCTION TIME**
**FROM FURNACE TO FINISHED BOTTLE: AT LEAST 24 HOURS**

**11 At the warehouse** Bottles are packed into pallets, then moved on rails to the warehouse. Here they wait to be loaded onto trucks and taken to stores for sale.

THE END

...contain **at least 50% recycled glass.**

>>

**Here you can see** just one area of an enormous bottle-making factory, where bottles are produced 24 hours a day, 365 days of the year. The factory makes up to a staggering four million bottles every day.

>>

**Most of the work** is done by machines. This man's job is to check the quality of the bottles, so he is collecting samples for inspection. Other people who work in the factory are maintenance engineers who look after the machines, and supervisors who make sure everything runs smoothly.

<<

**Accumulation tables** give bottles somewhere to go when production has to stop for maintenance.

This factory has two huge furnaces...

**It takes an hour** for the bottles to pass through the lehrs. Here they are heated, then slowly cooled to room temperature. As the lehrs are enclosed, the bottles cool on both the inside and outside at the same time. This process (called annealing) makes them less likely to shatter.

DID YOU KNOW?

This factory and warehouse are longer than five football fields laid end to end.

**Conveyor belts** The bottles leave the lehr and travel 12 deep on conveyor belts. They move along at an average walking speed of 4 mph 6 (km/h).

...each about the Size of a four-bedroom house.

# Glossary

**aluminum**
A lightweight silvery metal that conducts heat and electricity well. Aluminum is widely used in manufacturing.

**bar code**
A system of parallel lines (printed on goods) that a computer can read to gain information, including price.

**binary**
A system of numbers that uses only 0 and 1.

**binder**
The material that gives paint its texture and consistency.

**block**
The stiffened toe of a ballet dancer's pointe shoe.

**blowpipe**
Tool used by glass blowers to turn molten glass into shaped objects.

**boll**
The fluffy white seedpod of a cotton plant, which is harvested to make cotton fabric.

**casing**
The edible skin of a sausage.

**clicker**
A skilled worker who is responsible for cutting most of the elements of a pointe shoe out of leather, thin wood, or cardboard.

**collate**
To collect in a particular order.

**conching**
A final step in the chocolate-making process, conching mixes, kneads, and massages the chocolate mixture for a long time to make it taste and feel smooth.

**conveyor belt**
A constantly moving surface that takes parts or finished objects from one place to another in a manufacturing process.

**cure**
To preserve by drying or smoking.

**digital**
Relating to information that is given, stored, or worked with in the form of numbers.

**emulsify**
To blend tiny droplets of one liquid into another liquid.

**fire**
To bake pottery in a special oven called a kiln.

**gob**
A lump of liquid glass ready to be made into a glass or a bottle.

**granules**
Small, hard particles that are sometimes melted to make manufactured objects. Plastic blocks start life as granules.

**hive**
A place where lots of bees live, and where they store their honey.

**homogenize**
To reduce the size of the particles in a substance so they are small and evenly distributed.

**injection molding**
Shaping heated material by placing it into a mold during the manufacture of plastic or rubber objects.

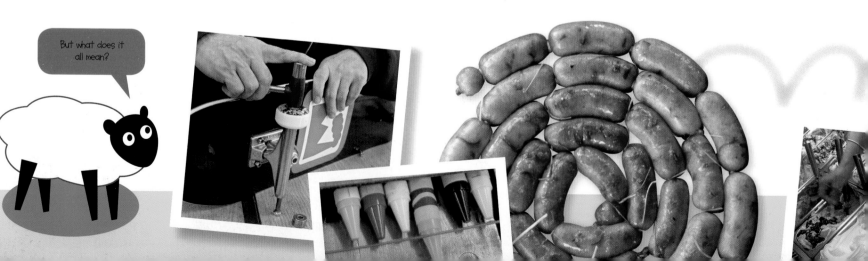

But what does it all mean?

**laner**
A machine that arranges massed objects into an orderly line during a production process.

**laser**
An intense, narrow beam of light or radiation.

**last**
A model of a foot used by shoemakers.

**lehr**
A cooling tunnel for glass.

**mill**
This word can mean "grind," as in grinding wheat to make flour, or "mix around," as in milling binder and pigment in paint.

**molten**
Something made liquid by heating.

**mute**
This word describes a creature that is not able to make sounds through its mouth.

**nectar**
The sweet liquid found in flowers that is collected by bees.

**pasteurize**
To bring a substance to a high temperature to kill germs.

**pigment**
The material that gives paint or dye its color. Pigments can be natural or man-made.

**plastic**
A man-made material that can be molded when it's warm, but usually remains solid or slightly bendable when it's cool.

**pollen**
The fine dust produced by flowers that makes it possible for one flower to fertilize another.

**pomology**
The science of growing apples.

**recycle**
To avoid waste by reusing part, or all, of an object for its original purpose, or for a different purpose.

**resin**
One of several yellowish/brown plant secretions (amber, for example) that don't dissolve in

water, and are used in the making of varnishes, inks, and plastics.

**temper**
To mix a substance very well so it's the same texture throughout.

**template**
A pattern used as a guide for cutting or drawing a shape.

**transfer**
A picture or design that is transferred from one surface (often paper) to another by contact.

**truss rod**
The metal strengthening strip along the neck of an electric guitar.

# Index

From apple juice to T-shirts, now you know how everything is made!

Goodbye

# Acknowledgments

The publisher would like to thank the following for their kind permission to reproduce their pictures:

(Key: a-above; b-below/bottom; c-center; f-far; l-left; r-right; t-top)

**Alamy Images:** Ron Buskirk 48bl; Buzz Pictures 40l; Chuck Cecil/AGStockUSA, Inc. 52tl; Keith Dannemiller 53tl; Fenix Rising 48clb, 48crb, 49bl; Peter Griffin 89bl; D. Hurst 4-5b, 66bl; Neil McAllister 15; Diana Mewes/Cephas Picture Library 88bl; Steve Sant 1clb, 14tr; toto 11; Visual Arts Library (London) 14clb. **Ardea:** Pascal Goetgheluck 7cb. **Cheap Trick:** 63br. **Corbis:** Evans Caglage/Dallas Morning News 5fbr, 34bl; China Newsphoto/ Reuters 41tr; Gianni Dagli Orti 70tr; Owen Franken 10br; Michael Freeman 22c; Historical Picture Archive/Philip de Bay 11cl; Mimmo Jodice 10cb; Yiorgos Karahalis/Reuters 71tr; National Gallery Collection; By kind permission of the Trustees of the National Gallery, London 6tr; Reuters 19tr; Kevin Schafer 52bl; Phil Schermeister 5bl, 63bc; Schultheiss Productions/ Zefa 51bc; Ted Streshinsky 14br; Michael S. Yamashita 48br. **DK Images:** Lindsey Stock 88bc (glasses); Judith Miller/Jeanette Hayhurst Fine Glass 10crb; Judith Miller/T W Conroy 7ca; Judith Miller/Woolley and Wallis 66fbr; Natural History Museum, London 66cla; Odds Farm Park, High Wycombe, Bucks 24tl; Stephen Oliver 11clb (cornet), 13cra, 66bc, 94br (ice cream); Oxford Scientific Films 44br, 46br; Rough Guides 13br, 26cr; The Science Museum, London 48cra (gunpowder); Jerry Young 46tc (bee). **FLPA:** David Hosking 22tr, 94tr. **Getty Images:** The Bridgeman Art Library/Friedrich Heinrich Fuger 75tr; The Bridgeman Art Library/Italian School 10tl; The Bridgeman Art Library/Richard Bridges Beechey 71tl (boats); The Image Bank/Dave Nagel 31ca; The Image Bank/Peter Dazeley 3tc, 58l, 59cb, 95tc; Lonely Planet Images/Paul Kennedy 40tr; Photographer's Choice/Frank Cezus 45, 46c; Photographer's Choice/Joe McBride 3bc, 41cb; Photographer's Choice/Michael Rosenfeld 10bl, 56cl; Riser/Thomas Northcut 71ca, 73tc; Stone/Pier 1crb, 61br; Taxi 31; Taxi Japan/Masaaki Toyoura 35 (b/g); Taxi/Nick Clements 41 (b/g). **Photolibrary:** Anthony Blake 53bl, 53cl, 53tr, 94bl (hands). **PunchStock:** Burke/Triolo Productions/Brand X 25tr; Digital Vision/Thomas Northcut 63tc; Image Source Pink 5r (juice), 36cl; Photodisc 5clb, 42tl. **Science Photo Library:** Bill Barksdale/Agstockusa 48c, 50tc; Dr. Jeremy Burgess 30tr; Scott Camazine 44bl; Getmapping PLC 66tl; Russell Graves/Agstockusa 49; Library Of Congress 88tl; Andrew J. Martinez 80tr; Ann Pickford 80fcrb; Malkolm Warrington 70tl, 72tc.

**Jacket images:** Front: **Corbis:** Al Fuchs/NewSport fbl. Back: **DK Images:** Stephen Oliver tc (ice cream). Spine: **DK Images:** Stephen Oliver c; Rotring UK Ltd. b.

All other images © Dorling Kindersley
For further information see: www.dkimages.com

Every effort has been made to trace the copyright holders. Dorling Kindersley apologizes for any unintentional omissions and would be pleased, in any such cases, to add an acknowledgment in future editions.

For making this book possible, Dorling Kindersley would like to thank:

**Winsor & Newton** (oil paints)
**Marine Ices** (ice cream)
**Dartington Crystal** (blown glass)
**Freed of London** (pointe shoes)
**Tablehurst Farm** (sausages)
**LEGO** (plastic blocks)
**Media Sourcing** (compact discs)
**Copella** (apple juice)
**A Third Foot, Ideal Skateboards** (skateboard)
**Ethically Sourced Products, Discovery Knitting, Colours Dyers and Finishers** (cotton T-shirt)
**L'Artisan du Chocolat** (chocolate)
**Cumberland Pencil Company** (pencils)
**J J Guitars** (electric guitar)
**Burgess Dorling and Leigh** (ceramic mug)
**Master Ropemakers** (rope)
**Westcombe Dairy** (cheese)
**Soapworks, The Body Shop** (soap)
**Crayola** (crayons)
**Quinn Glass, Britvic, Fentimans** (glass bottle)

Dorling Kindersley would also like to thank: Ted Hobday from the Brogdale Agricultural Trust for information about apple varieties; Robbie Jack for special photography of The Royal Ballet shoe room; Rob Nunn, Rose Horridge, and Claire Bowers for picture research; Gemma Fletcher for design assistance; Zahavit Shalev and Elizabeth Haldane for editorial assistance.

We hope you've enjoyed seeing how things are made—we've certainly enjoyed showing you the ropes!